Narrative of the
Most Extraordinary and Distressing

SHIPWRECK OF THE WHALESHIP *ESSEX*

Owen Chase

With supplementary accounts
of survivors and Herman Melville's
memoranda on Owen Chase

Foreword by Tim Cahill
Introduction by Paul Lyons

THE LYONS PRESS

Originally published in 1821 by W. B. Gilley as *Narrative
of the Most Extraordinary and Distressing Shipwreck of the
Whale-ship* Essex, *of Nantucket; which was attacked and
finally destroyed by a large spermaceti-whale, in the Pacific
Ocean; with an account of the unparalleled sufferings of the
captain and crew during a space of ninety-three days at sea,
in open boat; in the years 1819 & 1820.*

First Lyons Press edition, 1999

10 9 8 7 6 5 4 3 2 1

The Library of Congress Cataloging-in-Publication Data
Chase, Owen.
    Shipwreck of the whaleship Essex / Owen Chase ;
foreword by Tim Cahill.—1st Lyons Press ed.
        p.   cm.
    "Originally published in 1821 by W. B. Gilley"—
T.p. verso.
    ISBN 1-55821-878-5 (pbk.)
    1. Essex (Whale-ship)   I. Title.
G530.E72   1999
910.4′5—dc21   99-24889
                                                    CIP

CONTENTS

FOREWORD

ON November 20, 1820, the whaling vessel *Essex,* out of Nantucket, spotted a "shoal" of sperm whales. It was a fine clear day, about eight in the morning. The ship lay off the west coast of the Americas, just south of the equator, almost equidistant from the Galapagos Islands and the Marquesas Islands, some-times referred to as the islands farthest from any continent on earth. Two whaling boats, very lightly built for rowing speed, were lowered from the *Essex.* The crew pursued and harpooned three of the whales when the largest of the cetaceans, a creature some eighty-five feet long, rammed the vessel not once but twice in the space of ten minutes, and "stove in her bows." All twenty hands survived the attack and assembled in three of the "fragile" whal-ing boats, the very ones used to chase and kill whales. The *Essex* itself slowly rolled onto her mast and, over the space of two days, sunk. The crew had time to recover some bread and several kegs of drinking water, along with necessary navigational equipment.

Sailing some three months and three thousand miles in the flimsy open boats, the whalers suffered terribly from thirst and hunger. Only eight men sur-vived the ordeal. One of the three boats was lost at sea. Six of the men who died of hunger and thirst were eaten by survivors, in order to sustain life.

An account of the "unparalleled sufferings of the captain and crew" was written a year later by one of the survivors, Owen Chase, then twenty-three years old, first mate on the *Essex*. The book was little read in its time, and never reprinted, though the story of the *Essex* and the vengeful whale who sunk her circulated through the whaling community in Nantucket. Some twenty years after the publication of the book, Herman Melville borrowed a copy of the narrative from the son of Owen Chase, and read it on a whaling vessel plying the South Pacific. "The reading of the wondrous story upon the landless sea and close to the very latitude of the shipwreck had a surprising effect on me." Eight years later, Melville began writing *Moby Dick*.

That the narrative of Owen Chase was an inspiration for Melville's masterpiece is undeniable. Modern readers, possessed of sensibilities and sympathies foreign to whalers of Chase's time, will likely find a certain poetic justice in the tragedy. Chase himself seems dimly aware of this: "I began to reflect on the . . . deadly attack . . . by an animal, too, never before suspected of pre-meditated violence and proverbial for its inoffensiveness." The attacks on the ship, Chase states, "were calculated to do us the most injury, by combining the speed of the two objects." The whale's "aspect was most horrible and such as indicated resentment and fury. He came directly from the shoal which we had just before entered, and, in which we had struck three of his companions, as if fired with revenge for their sufferings."

The reader who wishes to compare the destruction of the fictional *Pequod* with the historic *Essex* may conclude that Herman Melville stacked the metaphysical deck. The *Pequod*, for instance, was on a sealing expedition. No other whales were struck, and the great white whale's fury is made to seem wholly malevolent. It was perhaps necessary that readers' sympathies not be unduly divided.

Melville, in his notes on the narrative of Owen Chase, included here, suggests the book must have been written for Chase, but very probably from his direct narration off the "nine or ten scraps of paper" on which he kept notes. Indeed, much of the prose seems stiffly posed, as in a portrait painted by a journeyman artist, skilled in detail but lacking in inspiration. The authors are careful to commit nothing that may be considered philosophy—aside from several nods towards divine providence—and the reader is obliged, willy-nilly, to consider various aspects of morality. What makes one man strive to survive when others give up and wait for death? Is a passive suicide preferable to endurance of endless suffering?

Melville was not interested in the epic journey in open boats across storm-tossed seas—a feat of navigation and survival that rivals those of Shackleton and Bligh. The sailors might have set out to the west and made for the Marquesas (or Tahiti), but feared—incorrectly as it turned out—they might there become the victims of cannibals. The irony, not specifically commented upon by Chase but mentioned by Melville, is that, by sailing southeast to

Chile, they compounded their own misery, which included the painful decision to consume the bodies of their deceased companions. (Indeed, in a second boat, lots were drawn and an unfortunate young man voluntarily offered himself up to be shot in order to feed his fellows). Fear of cannibalism drove them to cannibalism.

Various aspects of the Chase narrative make for fearful and compulsive reading. In the latter stages of the voyage, the men lived in such proximity to death that each successive breath must have required an act of will. Two men on Chase's boat chose to die, announcing this determination ahead of time. Then they lay down and were dead within a day. These men were buried at sea. Later, to save themselves, the survivors ate the remains of the third man to die. Chase precisely describes the disposition of the body, and one learns this rather hideous fact: On short rations, it takes three men seven days to consume the flesh of another human being.

The present volume contains two missionary tracts. South Seas missionaries of the day collected tales of privation and debauchery among indigenous peoples: It was a kind of tabloid pamphleteering in the interest of salvation. The first tract is the statement of Captain Pollard, who commanded the only other surviving whale boat from the *Essex,* and which contains an account of the decision to draw lots in the life or death lottery. The second tract is a short account of three men from the *Essex* who made the decision to remain on a small island the whale boats

had encountered. Chase and Pollard found almost
no fresh water, and very little to eat. They chose to
sail on. The men who remained on the island sought
shelter from the elements in a cave, where they
encountered the skeletons of eight men, probably
marooned sailors like themselves. This is the stuff of
great ghost stories, made all the more terrifying
because it is surely the truth. The three men were
subsequently rescued.

There are certain discrepancies among the various
accounts of the shipwreck and subsequent voyage,
but it is the narrative of Owen Chase that one comes
to trust. There is a certain stalwart honesty in this
book that was admittedly written "in the hope of
obtaining something of remuneration." In fact, it
inspired one of the great masterpieces of American
literature, and, even today, one can hardly read it
without imagining that there is at least one more
great novel buried, gemlike, somewhere in its won-
derfully stiff and stoic prose.

TIM CAHILL
March 15, 1999

INTRODUCTION

I

[Nantucket] seems to have been inhabited merely to
prove what mankind can do.

—Hector St. John de Crevecouer
Description of the Island of Nantucket

THE narrative of the wreck of the *Essex* of Nantucket, as told by the first mate of the *Essex,* Owen
Chase, is a Nantucket story. Anchored to the history
of the whale fishery and America's economic expansion, its principal actors embody a Nantucket world
view, with all its pious industry and perseverance. And
it is ultimately a story about what mankind can do.

Owen Chase, the only one of the *Essex*'s eight survivors to write an extended account of the wreck,
and thus its primary historian, was a dyed-in-the-wool
Yankee. His paternal ancestor landed with Governor
Winthrop in 1630, and his maternal ancestors were
among those late seventeenth-century Quakers who,
disgruntled with the mainland Puritan theocracy,
decided to resettle on the sandy island of Nantucket.
They were thrifty and hard working, living off what

the sea provided. On his mother's side Chase was a distant relation to Benjamin Franklin.

The early Nantucketers integrated whaling methods learned from Native Americans with their own (crews often included Native Americans), and extracted oil from whale blubber on tryworks erected on the beach. The Nantucketers used the whole whale; bone was used to make women's hoopskirts, waxy spermaceti to make candles or salves. By the eighteenth century Nantucket had become synonymous with whaling, and the combination of the islanders' plain, enterprising brand of Quakerism and the daily trials of the sea forged a particular Nantucket character and salty idiom.

Nantucket whaling grounds expanded dramatically after 1712, when Captain Christopher Hussey's ship was blown by a storm beyond the customary Nantucket fishing limits, and Hussey fell in with a school of sperm whales and managed to kill one. Sperm whales—which yielded a superior quantity and grade of oil—had been thought of as rare and hard to take, and fishing had stayed close to shore. Within a few years of Hussey's catch whaling ports sprung up all along the eastern seaboard, and captains were chasing sperm whales around the world, charting the currents, surveying coastlines, and establishing trading posts. Whaling was the new frontier, the vanguard industry that carried America into the Pacific.

Greater distances meant longer voyages—generally of two to four years. In *Moby Dick,* Herman Melville writes of a character named Bulkington for whom "the land seemed scorching to his feet." There were many Bulkingtons in the Nantucket fishery, men who would return and spend a month at home with their long-suffering wives, then take off again for the other side of the earth. It was not unusual for a whaler to have grown children, two to four years apart in age, that he had seen for a total of one year. The profits were great, and so were the perils. There was something of the fatalistic adventurer's spirit of cosmic gambling about these men who made their fortunes pursuing creatures twenty times the size of an elephant in small wooden boats—that and a deeply ingrained sense of their own hereditary intrepidness. "A Nantucket man is on all occasions fully sensible of the honor and merit of his profession," Owen Chase writes, "no doubt because he knows that his laurels, like the soldier's, are plucked from the brink of danger."

The whaling industry flourished until the American Revolution, during which the fleet was nearly wiped out, and many of its ablest seamen were lost at sea or imprisoned by the British. Thirty years later, when it had largely recovered, the fleet was decimated again during the War of 1812. The years following the end of that war saw an unprecedented expansion. New Bedford came to rival Nantucket as a whaling center, but with oil prices and demand rising there was plenty of room for both and a bustling need for labor. Ship builders and whaling crews increasingly included Portuguese, African Americans, Native Americans, and Pacific Islanders in particular. In his preface to the narrative, Chase describes the influx of capital into the recovered fishery as "energies burst out afresh." He alludes to the commercial and scientific benefits of the American presence in the Pacific, and appeals to Congress for "deserved government patronage" of whaling and naval protection. These contexts are not incidental to the narrative. Indeed, they speak to Chase's and his compatriots' providential sense of the importance of whaling to a broader American enterprise; as well as to their "shock" when—in an instant—their "pleasing anticipations" of profit are "dejected" by a "most mysterious, and overwhelming calamity."

II

Their lives have ever been one continual round of, hair-breadth escapes. . . . Many a tale of danger and toil and suffering, startling, severe, and horrible, has illumined the pages of the history of this pursuit, and scarce any, even the humblest of these hardy mariners, but can, from his own experience, narrate truths stranger than fiction.

—Alexander Starbuck
History of the American Whale Fishery (1877)

ON June 11, 1821, the *Eagle,* Captained by William H. Coffin, returned to Nantucket carrying four survivors of the wrecked whaleship *Essex:* Benjamin Lawrence, Thomas Nickerson, Charles Ramsdell, and

Owen Chase. Legend has it that the ship flew a black flag from its mainmast, indicative of death at sea, and that the crowds on the wharves solemnly parted before these men, who had been presumed lost and who had a true story to tell of suffering at sea that rivaled any recorded in fiction.

On August 12, 1819, the *Essex,* captained by George Pollard, had sailed from Nantucket with a crew of twenty-one for the South Pacific, outfitted for a two-and-a-half-year cruise. Fourteen of the crew were white Americans, six were African Americans, and one an Englishman. One sailor disembarked at a South American port. The rest were wrecked when a rogue whale stove the ship. The crew salvaged what it could from the wreck and divided into three boats. After five weeks they came upon Henderson Island (which they believed was Ducie Island), but found insufficient provisions. Three men decided to take their chances on the island and the rest shoved off. The boats eventually parted ways. It was two months before two of them were rescued, and by that time both boats had resorted to cannibalism. The third boat was never heard from again. Eight men survived, including the three on Henderson Island.

Nantucketers were accustomed to firsthand stories of shipwreck and privation. In a small whaling community, in which many were related by birth or marriage, nearly everyone had lost someone dear to them to a watery grave. The annals of the American whale fishery are full of matter-of-fact entries like "lost off the coast of Brazil with all on board," or, simply, "missing." Many stories of sailors who had survived storms, or fallen among pirates, or lived for a time among Pacific Islanders were "got up" by literary hacks, so that by the 1820s "yarns" were becoming a Nantucket commodity along with scrimshaw and oil. As Owen Chase recognized in his address "To the Reader," "the public mind [had] been already nearly sated with the private stories of individuals."

Even in such a climate of inflated storytelling the tale of the *Essex* was recognized as extraordinary. Almost immediately penny ballads about the wreck began to circulate through whaling ports. The sensation that the story caused no doubt contributed to Owen Chase's decision to assemble the narrative for publication shortly after his return. He tells the reader with Nantucket directness that he had lost a great deal financially in the wreck, and felt he might obtain "something of remuneration, by giving a short history of [his] sufferings to the world."

There is no evidence, inside the narrative or out, that Chase had any hankering after literary reputation. From reading his imperfectly literate ship logs for later voyages, it is clear that he never would have achieved any if it had not been for the narrative. Chase claims that while at sea he "commenced to keep a sort of journal with the little paper and pencil which I had," and these notes were no doubt useful in preparing the narrative along with an unknown literary hack, who Chase employed as sailors with stories to tell generally did. Whoever this hack was, he seems to stick close to Chase's facts and sensibility. "There seems no reason to suppose that Owen himself wrote the Narrative," Herman Melville commented. "It bears obvious tokens of having been written for him; but at the same time, its whole air plainly evinces that it was carefully & [conscientiously] written to Owen's dictation of facts.—It is almost as good as tho' Owen wrote it himself."

The narrative gains force from this air of genuineness. Its bare-bones language is all the more stirring and dramatic for not seeming, in most places, to strain after effect. The language is extraordinary where it is simply adequate to an extraordinary reality. As Chase says, "the facts contained in this little volume" are not "so extravagant, as to require the exercise of any great credulity." His account of the limits of human endurance does not have to be imagined and embellished because it has been lived through. What can today seem a formulaic rhetoric of extreme highs and lows ("unparalleled sufferings," as the title page puts it), punctuated by expressions of ejaculatory piety, are generic features of shipwreck narrative that no one writing after Defoe's *Robinson Crusoe* seemed able to avoid. If in its more graphic moments—with its mention of "flesh that had become tainted, and had turned of a greenish colour"—the narrative reminds readers of passages in Edgar Allan Poe, it is because Poe, in particular in *The Narrative of Arthur Gordon Pym of Nantucket* (1838), plunders many such details directly from Chase's narrative.

There is no evidence that Chase was well-remunerated for his narrative labors, as the limited edition of the narrative was not reprinted during Chase's lifetime. In the 1830s, accounts of the *Essex* resurfaced in numerous popular articles, religious tracts, mariner's chronicles, and school books, including McGuffey's *Fourth Eclectic Reader,* from which a generation of the nation's students received instruction. Of the tales of danger and toil and suffering from the early whale fishery that have survived into the twentieth century, the wreck of the *Essex* has arguably had the greatest staying power: It has been the subject of a *Life Magazine* feature, a novel—Henry Carlisle's *The Jonah Man* (1984)—and a full-scale museum exhibit, to name just a few examples. The narrative surfaces regularly in American literature—in places like Ralph Waldo Emerson's journals and letters or Walt Whitman's poetry—and it breaches most spectacularly in Herman Melville's writing.

III

As if to strike terror into them, by this time being the first assailant himself, Moby Dick turned, and was now coming for the three crews.
— Herman Melville, *Moby Dick*

IN addition to the unprecedented time spent on the open sea—which nearly doubled the forty-eight days of Captain Bligh's famous ordeal in an open boat after the mutiny on the *Bounty*—two facts stood out in the story of the wreck of the *Essex*. The ship had been stove, seemingly deliberately, by a whale, and in the aftermath the crew had resorted to cannibalism to survive. The first fact was the more remarkable, since in the history of whaling up until that time there had been no recorded instance of a whale maliciously attacking a ship. Chase's reaction to what he calls a "hitherto unheard of circumstance" includes metaphysical bewilderment:

> I began to reflect on the accident, and endeavored to realize by what unaccountable destiny or design, (which I could not at first determine,), this sudden and most deadly attack had been made upon us: by an animal, too, never before suspected of premeditated violence, and proverbial for its insensibility and inoffensiveness. Every fact seemed to warrant me in concluding that it was any thing but chance which directed his operations.

Chase reiterates his sense of "decided, calculating mischief, on the part of the whale," and recalls how "the horrid aspect and revenge of the whale, wholly engrossed my attention."

Thirty years later, while working on *Moby Dick* (1851), Herman Melville underlined this passage in his copy of Chase's narrative, and marked and put a question mark next to Chase's later assertion that "There was not a hope now remaining to us but that which was derived from a sense of the mercies of the

Creator." What gripped Melville about the narrative was the idea of the supposedly gentle whale turning intelligently violent. This image was percolating in his imagination as early as *Mardi* (1848), when Melville wrote of how "the good craft *Essex,* and others, have been sunk by sea-monsters." Melville was struck too by Chase's Joblike sense of God testing the crew through the agency of a whale. In *Moby Dick,* Captain Ahab cannot accept his first mate's argument that Moby Dick "smote [him] from blindest instinct," and the penultimate chase chapters of the novel bear out this belief. Here Melville draws most heavily on Chase, as the albino whale—acting like the agent of some obscure divine force or historical principle—turns dazzlingly vindictive and splinters the doomed *Pequod.*

To set up his ending Melville earlier summarizes Chase's account of the whale's attack in *Moby Dick* (chapter 45): "The Sperm Whale is in some cases sufficiently powerful, knowing, and judiciously malicious, as with direct aforethought to stave in . . . a large ship; and what is more, the Sperm Whale has done it." Throughout the book he amplifies on Chase's "calculating" whale by attributing to Moby Dick "craft," "intent," "malicious intelligence," and "eternal malice." The finale of *Moby Dick* echoes Chase's metaphors, nautical orders, location, and details of the whale's attack: In each story the whale attacks twice, striking the ship on the starboard bow. The last words of the crew in *Moby Dick,* "The ship? Great God, where is the ship?" virtually quote the reaction to the wreck in Chase's narrative, "Oh, my God! Where is the ship?"

Part of what has allowed Chase's narrative to be read as more than a story of remarkable human will to survive—which it of course is—is the literary use Herman Melville made of it. Chase's narrative has, in many circles, become forever spliced to Melville's as a kind of literary footnote. This would be unfortunate were it not that Melville draws out much of the poetry and philosophical suggestiveness of the narrative that might otherwise remain hidden, because of both its generally matter-of-fact style and the ways in which the narrative has otherwise been read. For instance, when the narrative was included in widely read educational texts like McGuffey's *Fourth Eclectic Reader,* it was made to tell a conventional religious lesson.

Melville makes striking and visible in the narrative its complex qualities of classical tragedy, of an existential contest between humans and the inscrutable nature of things. "After the severest exposure, part of the crew reached the land in their boats," Melville writes of the *Essex* survivors in *Moby Dick.* "Exposure" to what, one asks. Melville deliberately avoids mentioning the crew's cannibalism, as did many nineteenth-century historians. While wind and sea and sun are brutal without protection, one must imagine that Melville extends the word "exposure" to cosmic senses as well.

The story of the *Essex* and its principals was as important to Melville as the printed narrative. Melville's fascination with Chase—whose name he always spelled "Chace"—and the events of the wreck is most evident in an eighteen-page memorandum entitled "What I Know of Owen Chace" (see page

119) found inside Melville's marked copy of the narrative. According to the memorandum on Chase, Melville first discussed the wreck of the *Essex* on the *Acushnet* in "forecastle conversation" in 1841. The second mate had sailed with Owen Chase, and spoke highly of him, but disappointed Melville in "not knowing more about the wreck than anyone else." That same year, the *Acushnet* gammed with another Nantucket ship, and Melville met Owen Chase's son at sea: "I questioned him concerning his father's adventure," Melville writes, "and when I left his ship to return again the next morning . . . he went to his chest & handed me a complete copy . . . the reading of this wondrous story upon the landless sea, & close to the very latitude of the shipwreck had a surprising effect on me." This was the beginning of a lifelong fascination with the events of the wreck and the effects on its survivors. Central types in Melville's work—the "castaway," the Jonah figure, the metaphysically afflicted man—resonate against the survivors of the *Essex*.

IV

At length one whispered his companion, who
   Whispered another, and thus it went round,
And then into a hoarser murmur grew,
   An ominous, and wild, and desperate sound;
And when his comrade's thought each sufferer knew,
   'Twas but his own, supressed till now, he found:

And out they spoke of lots for flesh and blood,
And who should die to be his fellow's food.

—George Gordon Lord Byron, *Don Juan*

THE cannibalism that the survivors of the *Essex* were driven to was a principal point of interest in the story—stories involving cannibalism, like that of the Donner Party or the survivors described in Piers Paul Read's best-selling *Alive* have always had a morbid popularity. But cannibalism at sea was hardly unprecedented. As recently as 1816 the crew of the wrecked French ship *Meduse* had engaged in cannibalism, and this had been the subject of both a written account by A. Correard and J. B. H. Savigny (London, 1818) and the lurid Theodore Gericault painting, *The Raft of the Medusa*. Every sailor who went to sea carried along stories of seamen who had been driven to "the last horrible extremity." Many popular ballads describing wrecks even contained what might be considered instruction for eventualities at sea, legitimating a "code of conduct" in which it would be acceptable for "one to be sacrificed to save the rest."

Less conceptually acceptable to Westerners was the idea of winding up in a savage "cannibal pot." Wild tales about cannibalism circulated onboard ships as "yarns"—sometimes told by captains to discourage potential deserters, as in Melville's first novel, *Typee* (1846). These accounts moved from nautical ballads and ship narratives into many popular forms, from nursery rhymes to poems and literary narratives. Jonathan Swift, for instance, wrote quite conventionally in *The South Sea Project* (1721) that "A savage race, by shipwrecks fed,/Lie waiting for the foundered skiffs,/And strip the bodies of the dead."

This notion that Pacific Islanders were rapacious cannibals had an exorbitant, phobic hold on the Western imagination, with little basis in fact. Chase writes that the crew believed that in Tahiti there were savages "from whom we had as much to fear, as from the elements, or even death itself." The narrative illustrates how far Westerners could be driven by their obsessive fear of native cannibalism, and how the yarns circulating in and about the Pacific fishery fed fantasy and influenced behavior. In this case the crew of the *Essex* journeyed thousands of miles out of their way and wound up committing the very act that they feared. The irony struck Herman Melville, who noted in the Chase memorandum:

—All the sufferings of these miserable men of the Essex might, in all human probability, have been avoided, had they, immediately after leaving the wreck, steered straight for Tahiti, from which they were not very distant at the time, & to which, there was a fair Trade wind. But they dreaded cannibals, & strange to tell knew not that for more than 20 years, the English missionaries had been resident in Tahiti; & that in the same year of the shipwreck—1820—it was entirely safe for the mariner to touch at Tahiti. But they chose to stem a head wind, & make a passage of several thousand miles . . . in order to gain a civilised harbor on the coast of South America.

Even Melville's memorandum suggests that had
sailors landed in Tahiti before the arrival of missionaries, there might have been good reason to
fear being eaten by cannibals. In fact, with rare
exceptions involving actual or symbolic ingestion of
eyeballs by chiefs, cannibalism was not part of
Tahitian culture. The Pacific archive reveals that,
prior to the colonial period, Tahitians generally
showed Westerners great hospitality. This is the
point that Melville stresses in his later treatment of
the *Essex* in *Clarel* (1876), where he reiterates: "the
isles were dreaded—every chain;/Better to brave
the immense of sea,/And venture for the Spanish
Main," and concludes, "So deemed he, strongly er-
ring there."

The generally agreed-upon procedure when cannibalism at sea became necessary was the drawing of
lots. This was in keeping with biblical sortilege—the
dependence on what looks like chance to know the
will of God. Drawing lots scripted the scene of disaster as a theological event, outside of the ship's
normal systems of power and hierarchy. In a survival
situation, in theory, the captain and the crew were
to be seen as equals in the eyes of God. In Chase's
boat Chase, Benjamin Lawrence, and Thomas Nicholson
survived by eating the bodies of men who had died
of starvation. In Pollard's boat it eventually became
necessary to draw lots, and Charles Ramsdell (spelled
"Ramsdale" in the narrative) ultimately shot Owen
Coffin, Pollard's nephew. In Pollard's account he
says, "My lad, my lad, if you don't like your lot, I'll
shoot the first man that touches you."

One might question the lot of the six African-American sailors: None survived and four seem to have died in rapid succession and been consumed before the drawing of lots became necessary. Was this a coincidence, the result of the allotments of food prior to, or after, the wreck? There are examples, like the wreck of the *Peggy* (1765), in which an African slave was said, improbably, to have drawn the unlucky lot. Such questions have never, to my knowledge, been asked about the aftermath of the wreck of the *Essex,* and are ultimately unanswerable. Chase's "Narrative," with its emphasis throughout on situation, logistics, and Providence over characterization, gives no sense that the African-Americans in the boats were treated differently from the rest of the crew—Quakers had always opposed slavery, and African-Americans often found more equitable treatment in the fishery than elsewhere.

There is no record of the *Essex* survivors being questioned about anything that happened in the boats; Pollard was never held to account for allowing the murder of his nephew Owen Coffin. (In the later case of the *Mignonette,* two men who matter-of-factly admitted to drawing lots and shooting a fellow sailor in order to survive were put on trial and convicted.) The experience no doubt told hard on the survivors, none of whom in later life were much disposed to discuss the wreck. In his interview with the missionary George Bennet, several years after the tragedy, Captain Pollard breaks off after his description of cannibalism with the words "But I can tell you no more—my head is on fire at the recollection; I hardly know what to say."

V

After such knowledge, what forgiveness?
—T. S. Eliot, "Gerontion"

ALL five Nantucket survivors of the wreck of the *Essex* went back to sea. Chase eventually became the captain of the whaler *Charles Carroll* (1832), and twice returned from the Pacific with his holds full of sperm oil. In later life he was said to have developed an obsessive fear of starvation, never wasting a morsel at the dinner table, and frequenting the market to buy supplies that he larded in his attic.

George Pollard was given command on the very Nantucket whaler, *The Two Brothers,* that had brought him back to Nantucket after his rescue. Charles Wilkes writes in his *Autobiography* of having discussed the wreck with Pollard, asking him how he "could think of again putting his foot on board ship," to which Pollard "simply remarked that it was an old adage that lightning never struck in the same place twice." But the unfortunate captain ran aground and wrecked his new command near the Hawaiian Islands, and spent a few days in an open boat before being picked up by a whaler. "Now I am utterly ruined," he told Bennet on his passage back to Nantucket. "No owner will ever trust me with a whaler again, for all will say that I am an unlucky man." After returning to Nantucket in 1825, he became a night watchman.

The image of Pollard pacing the decks at night, unable to protect his crew at sea, determined to make his contribution to public safety on the docks, seems to have stayed latest and deepest with Herman Melville. In the Chase memorandum he writes that he "saw Capt. Pollard on the island of Nantucket, and exchanged some words with him. To the islanders he was a nobody—to me, the most impressive man, tho' wholly unassuming, even humble, I ever encountered." In *Moby Dick* Melville writes, "Being returned home at last, Captain Pollard once more sailed for the Pacific in command of another ship, but the gods shipwrecked him again." A note in his journals for 1856–57 reads simply: "Cap. Pollard. of Nant." These journals record the experiences of religious questioning that Melville was to work into *Clarel,* a section of which depicts the chastened figure of Pollard pacing the docks:

> A Jonah is he?—And men bruit
> The story. None will give him place
> In a third venture. Came the day
> Dire need constrained the man to pace
> A night patrolman on the quay
> Watching the bales till morning hour
> Through fair and foul. Never he smiled;
> Call him, and he would come; not sour
> In spirit, but meek and reconciled;

Oft on some secret thing would brood.
He ate what came, though but a crust;
In Calvin's creed he put his trust;
Praised heaven, and said that God was good,
And his calamity but just.

BIBLIOGRAPHIC NOTE:
The best source of information about the wreck of the
Essex, of course, is Chase's narrative itself. Readers disposed to look further should begin with the most
thorough scholarly treatment, Thomas Heffernan's
excellent *Stove By a Whale: Owen Chase and the Essex*
(1981, reprinted 1990); Heffernan includes a compre-
hensive discussion and assessment of the numerous
retellings of the *Essex* in the nineteenth and twentieth
centuries. In assembling this introduction, I have also
drawn in particular upon Alexander Starbuck's *History
of the Whale Fishery* (1877), Obed Macy's *History of
Nantucket* (1835), and upon introductions to previous
editions of *Shipwreck* by Robert Giddings (1935),
Edouard Stackpole (1950), R. B. McElderry Jr. (1963),
and Iola Haverstack and Betty Shephard (1965). The
Melville-Chase connection has been widely noted,
beginning with Raymond Weaver's *Herman Melville:
Mariner and Mystic* (1921); it is dramatically presented in Charles Olson's *Call Me Ishmael* (1947). For a
fascinating discussion of cannibalism and the codes
governing it on land and sea, see Brian Simpson's
*Cannibalism and the Common Law: The Story of the Tragic
Last Voyage of the Mignonette and the Strange Legal
Proceedings to Which it Gave Rise* (1984).

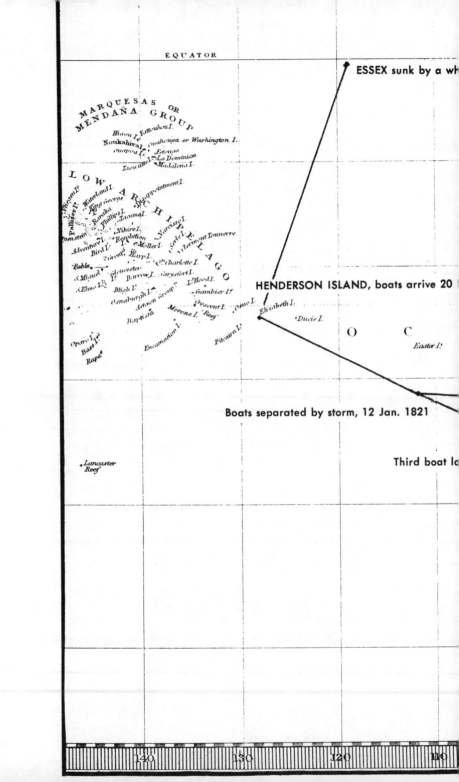

EQUATOR

ESSEX sunk by a wh

MARQUESAS OR
MENDAÑA GROUP

Hiaou I. Fattouhou I.
Nookahiva I. Ouaheuga or Washington I.
Ouapoa I. Fetouga
La Dominica
Trowa I. Madalena I.

LOW ARCHIPELAGO

Prince I.
Pallister I. Waterland I. Disappointment I.
King George
Romika
Phillips I. Tucamal.
Nihire I.
Adventure I. Resolution
Bird I. Moller I. Serle I. Clermont Tonnerre
Perrous Harp I.
Pablo
S. Miguel Gloucester O.te Charlotte I.
Barrow I. Carysfort I.
S. Elmo I. Bligh I. L.t Hood I.
Osnaburgh I. Gambier I.s
Acteon Group Prescent I. Oeno I.
Baptista Morone I. Reef Elizabeth I.

HENDERSON ISLAND, boats arrive 20

Pitcairn I. Ducie I.

O   C

Easter I.s

Opara I.
Bass I.
Rapa

Boats separated by storm, 12 Jan. 1821

Third boat la

Lancaster
Reef

140   130   120   110

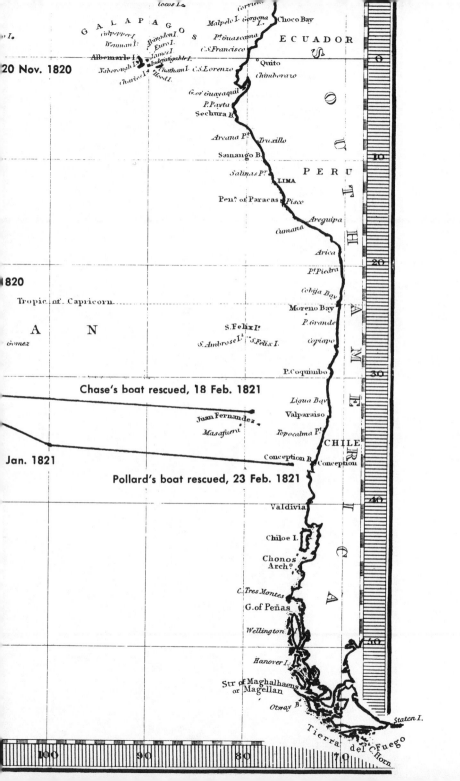

NARRATIVE

OF THE

MOST EXTRAORDINARY AND DISTRESSING

SHIPWRECK

OF THE

WHALE-SHIP ESSEX,

OF

NANTUCKET;

WHICH WAS ATTACKED AND FINALLY DESTROYED BY A LARGE

SPERMACETI-WHALE,

IN THE PACIFIC OCEAN;

WITH

AN ACCOUNT

OF THE

UNPARALLELED SUFFERINGS

OF THE CAPTAIN AND CREW

DURING A SPACE OF NINETY-THREE DAYS AT SEA, IN OPEN BOATS

IN THE YEARS 1819 & 1820

———

BY

OWEN CHASE,

OF NANTUCKET, FIRST MATE OF SAID VESSEL

———

NEW-YORK

PUBLISHED BY W. B. GILLEY, 92 BROADWAY

J. SEYMOUR, PRINTER

1821.

A Note on the Text

The text of the first edition of 1821 has been faithfully followed with the incorporation of the errata noted in the first edition, corrections of spelling, and minor punctuation changes.

TO THE READER

I AM aware that the public mind has been already nearly sated with the private stories of individuals, many of whom had few, if any, claims to public attention; and the injuries which have resulted from the promulgation of fictitious histories, and, in many instances, of journals entirely fabricated for the purpose, have had the effect to lessen the public interest in works of this description, and very much to undervalue the general cause of truth. It is, however, not the less important and necessary that narratives should continue to be furnished that have their foundations in fact; and the subject of which embraces new and interesting matter in any department of the arts or sciences. When the motive is worthy, the subject and style interesting, affording instruction, exciting a proper sympathy, and withal disclosing new and astonishing traits of human character:—this kind of information becomes of great value to the philanthropist and philosopher, and is fully deserving of attention from every description of readers.

On the subject of the facts contained in this little volume, they are neither so extravagant as to require the exercise of any great credulity to believe, nor, I trust, so unimportant or uninteresting as to forbid an attentive perusal. It was my misfortune to be a considerable, if not a principal, sufferer, in the dreadful catastrophe that befell us; and in it, I not only lost all the little I had ventured, but my situation and the prospects of bettering it, that at one time seemed to smile upon me, were all in one short moment destroyed with it. The hope of obtaining something of remuneration, by giving a short history of my sufferings to the world, must therefore constitute my claim to public attention.

PREFACE

THE increasing attention which is bestowed upon the whale fishery in the United States, has lately caused a very considerable commercial excitement; and no doubt it will become, if it be not at present, as important and general a branch of commerce as any belonging to our country. It is now principally confined to a very industrous and enterprising portion of the population of the states, many individuals of whom have amassed very rapid and considerable fortunes. It is a business requiring that labor, economy, and enterprise, for which the people of Nantucket are so eminently distinguished. It has enriched the inhabitants without bringing with it the usual corruptions and luxuries of a foreign trade; and those who are now most successful and conspicuous in it are remarkable for the primitive simplicity, integrity, and hospitality of the island. This trade, if I may so call it, took its rise amongst the earliest settlers, and has gradually advanced to the extended, important, and lucrative state in which it now is, without any material interruption, and with very little competition until the present time. The late war temporally, but in a great degree, affected its prosperity by subjecting numerous fine vessels with their cargoes to capture and loss; but in its short continuance it was not sufficient to divert the

energies of the capitalists embarked in it. At the conclusion of peace, those energies burst out afresh; and
our sails now almost whiten the distant confines of
the Pacific. The English have a few ships there; and
the advantages which they possess over ours, it may
be feared, will materially affect our success, by producing in time a much more extensive and powerful
competition. They are enabled to realize a greater
profit from the demand and price of oil in their mar-
kets; and the encouragement afforded by parliament,
not only in permitting the importation of it free of
duty, but in granting a liberal bounty. It is to be
hoped that the wisdom of Congress will be extended
to this subject; and that our present decided supre-
macy will not be lost for the want of a deserved government patronage.

Recent events have shown that we require a competent naval force in the Pacific for the protection of
this important and lucrative branch of commerce;
for the want of which, many serious injuries and in-
sults have been lately received, which have a ten-
dency to retard its flourishing progress, and which
have proved of serious consequence to the parties
concerned.

During the late war, the exertions and intrepidity
of Capt. Porter* were the means of saving a great
deal of valuable property, which otherwise must
have fallen into the hands of the enemy. His skillful,
spirited, and patriotic conduct, on all occasions
where he was called upon to act, imparted a protec-

* Captain David Porter of the United States frigate "Essex,"
1812-1814.

tion and confidence to our countrymen, which completely fulfilled their expectations of him, and without doubt those of the government in sending him there.

Our ships usually occupy from two to three years in making a voyage. Occasionally, necessity obliges them to go into port for provisions, water and repairs; in some cases, amongst mere savages, and in others, inhospitable people, from whom they are liable to every species of fraud, imposition, and force, which require some competent power to awe and redress. As long as the struggle between the patriots and royalists continues, or even should that speedily end —as long as young and instable governments, as there naturally must be for many years to come, exist there, our whalemen will continue to require that countenance and support which the importance and prosperity of the trade to them, and to the country, eminently entitle them. It is undoubtedly a most hazardous business; involving many incidental and unavoidable sacrifices, the severity of which it seems cruel to increase by the neglect or refusal of a proper protection.

The seamen employed in the fishery, and particularly those from Nantucket, are composed of the sons and connections of the most respectable families on the island; and, unlike the majority of the class or profession to which they belong, they labor not only for their temporary subsistence, but they have an ambition and pride among them which seeks after distinguishment and promotion. Almost all of them enter the service with views of a future command;

and submit cheerfully to the hardships and drud-
gery of the intermediate stations until they become
thoroughly acquainted with their business.

There are common sailors, boat-steerers, and har-
pooners: the last of these is the most honorable and
important. It is in this station that all the capacity of
the young sailor is elicited; on the dexterous management of the harpoon, the line, and the lance, and
in the adventurous positions which he takes alongside of his enemy, depends almost entirely the successful issue of his attack; and more real chivalry is
not often exhibited on the deck of a battle ship than
is displayed by these hardy sons of the ocean in some
of their gallant exploits among the whales. Nursed in
the dangers of their business, and exposed to the continual hazards and hardships of all seasons, climates,
and weathers, it will not be surprising if they should
become a fearless set of people, and pre-eminent in
all the requisites of good seamen. Two voyages are
generally considered sufficient to qualify an active
and intelligent young man for command; in which
time, he learns from experience, and the examples
which are set him, all that is necessary to be known.

While on this subject, I may be allowed to ob-
serve that it would not be an unprofitable task in
a majority of our respectable shipmasters in the
merchant service to look into the principles of
conduct, and study the economical management of
the captains of our whale-ships. I am confident many
serviceable hints could be gathered from the admirable system by which they regulate their concerns.
They would learn, also, what respect is due to the

character and standing of a captain of a whale-ship, which those of the merchant service affect so much to undervalue. If the post of danger be the post of honor; and if merit emanates from exemplary private character, uncommon intelligence, and professional gallantry, then is it due to a great majority of the shipmasters of Nantucket that they should be held above the operations of an invidious and unjust distinction. It is a curious fact that one does exist; and it is equally an illiberal, as an undeserved, reproach upon them, which time and an acquaintance with their merits must speedily wipe away.

NARRATIVE

CHAPTER I.

THE town of Nantucket, in the State of Massachusetts, contains about eight thousand inhabitants; nearly a third part of the population are quakers, and they are, taken together, a very industrious and enterprising people. On this island are owned about one hundred vessels, of all descriptions, engaged in the whale trade, giving constant employment and support to upwards of sixteen hundred hardy seamen, a class of people proverbial for their intrepidity. This fishery is not carried on to any extent from any other part of the United States, except from the town of New Bedford, directly opposite to Nantucket, where are owned probably twenty sail. A voyage generally lasts about two years and a half, and with an entire uncertainty of success. Sometimes they are repaid with speedy voyages and profitable cargoes, and at others they drag out a listless and disheartening cruise without scarcely making the expenses of an outfit. The business is considered a very hazardous one, arising from unavoidable accidents, in carrying on an exterminating warfare against those great leviathans of the deep; and indeed a Nantucket man is on all occasions fully sensible of the honor and merit of his profession; no doubt because he knows that his laurels, like the soldier's are plucked from the brink of danger. Numerous anecdotes are related of the

whalemen of Nantucket; and stories of hair-breadth
'scapes, and sudden and wonderful preservation are
handed down amongst them, with the fidelity, and no
doubt many of them with the characteristic fictions of
the ancient legendary tales. A spirit of adventure
amongst the sons of other relatives of those immediately concerned in it takes possession of their minds at
a very early age; captivated with the tough stories of
the elder seamen, and seduced as well by the natural
desire of seeing foreign countries, as by the hopes of
gain, they launch forth six or eight thousand miles
from home, into an almost untraversed ocean, and
spend from two to three years of their lives in scenes
of constant peril, labor, and watchfulness. The profession is one of great ambition, and full of honorable
excitement: a tame man is never known amongst
them; and the coward is marked with that peculiar
aversion that distinguishes our public naval service.
There are perhaps no people of superior corporeal
powers; and it has been truly said of them that they
possess a natural aptitude, which seems rather the
lineal spirit of their fathers than the effects of any experience. The town itself, during the war, was (naturally to have been expected) on the decline; but
with the return of peace it took a fresh start, and a
spirit for carrying on the fishery received a renewed
and very considerable excitement. Large capitals are
now embarked; and some of the finest ships that our
country can boast of are employed in it. The increased demand, within a few years past, from the
spermaceti manufactories, has induced companies and
individuals in different parts of the Union to become

engaged in the business; and if the future consumption of the manufactured article bear any proportion to that of the few past years, this species of commerce will bid fair to become the most profitable and extensive that our country possesses. From the accounts of those who were in the early stages of the fishery concerned in it, it would appear that the whales have been driven, like the beasts of the forest, before the march of civilization into remote and more unfrequented seas, until now they are followed by the enterprise and perseverance of our seamen even to the distant coasts of Japan.

The ship *Essex*, commanded by Captain George Pollard, Junior, was fitted out at Nantucket, and sailed on the 12th day of August, 1819, for the Pacific Ocean, on a whaling voyage. Of this ship I was first mate. She had lately undergone a thorough repair in her upper works, and was at that time, in all respects, a sound, substantial vessel: she had a crew of twenty-one men,* and was victualled and provided for two years and a half. We left the coast of America with a fine breeze, and steered for the Western Islands. On the second day out, while sailing moderately on our course in the Gulf Stream, a sudden squall of wind struck the ship from the S.W. and knocked her completely on her beam-ends, stove one of our boats, entirely destroyed two others, and threw down the cambouse.† We distinctly saw the approach of this gust, but miscalculated altogether as to the strength and

---

* Elsewhere, Chase refers to twenty, the number listed at the end of the *Narrative*.
† Variant of caboose.

violence of it. It struck the ship about three points
off the weather quarter, at the moment that the man
at the helm was in the act of putting her away to run
before it. In an instant she was knocked down with
her yards* in the water; and before hardly a moment
of time was allowed for reflection, she gradually came
to the wind, and righted. The squall was accompanied with vivid flashes of lightning and heavy and repeated claps of thunder. The whole ship's crew were,
for a short time, thrown into the utmost consternation and confusion; but fortunately the violence of
the squall was all contained in the first gust of the
wind, and it soon gradually abated, and became fine
weather again. We repaired our damage with little
difficulty, and continued on our course, with the loss
of the two boats. On the 30th of August we made the
island of Flores, one of the western group called the
Azores. We lay off and on the island for two days,
during which time our boats landed and obtained a
supply of vegetables and a few hogs: from this place
we took the N.E. trade wind, and in sixteen days
made the Isle of May, one of the Cape Verde. As we
were sailing along the shore of this island, we discovered a ship stranded on the beach, and from her
appearance took her to be a whaler. Having lost two
of our boats, and presuming that this vessel had probably some belonging to her that might have been
saved, we determined to ascertain the name of the
ship, and endeavour to supply if possible the loss of
our boats from her. We accordingly stood in towards
the port, or landing place. After a short time three

* Spars, slung crosswise to the mast.

men were discovered coming out to us in a whale boat. In a few moments they were alongside, and informed us that the wreck was the *Archimedes* of New York, Captain George B. Coffin, which vessel had struck on a rock near the island about a fortnight previously; that all hands were saved by running the ship on shore, and that the captain and crew had gone home. We purchased the whale boat of these people, obtained some more pigs, and again set sail. Our passage thence to Cape Horn was not distinguished for any incident worthy of note. We made the longitude of the Cape about the 18th of December, having experienced head winds for nearly the whole distance. We anticipated a moderate time in passing this noted land, from the season of the year at which we were there, being considered the most favourable; but instead of this, we experienced heavy westerly gales, and a most tremendous sea, that detained us off the Cape five weeks, before we had got sufficiently to the westward to enable us to put away. Of the passage of this famous Cape it may be observed that strong westerly gales and a heavy sea are its almost universal attendants: the prevalence and constancy of this wind and sea necessarily produce a rapid current, by which vessels are set to leeward; and it is not without some favourable slant of wind that they can in many cases get round at all. The difficulties and dangers of the passage are proverbial; but as far as my own observation extends (and which the numerous reports of the whalemen corroborate), you can always rely upon a long and regular sea; and although the gales may be very strong and stubborn, as they undoubtedly are,

they are not known to blow with the destructive violence that characterizes some of the tornadoes of the
western Atlantic Ocean. On the 17th of January,
1820, we arrived at the island of St. Mary's, lying on
the coast of Chili, in latitude 36° 59′ S., longitude 73°
41′ W. This island is a sort of rendezvous for whalers,
from which they obtain their wood and water, and
between which and the main land (a distance of
about ten miles) they frequently cruise for a species
of whale called the right whale. Our object in going
in there was merely to get the news. We sailed thence
to the island of Mas Afuera, where we got some wood
and fish, and thence for the cruising ground along the
coast of Chili, in search of the spermaceti whale. We
took there eight, which yielded us two hundred and
fifty barrels of oil; and the season having by this time
expired, we changed our cruising ground to the coast
of Peru. We obtained there five hundred and fifty
barrels. After going into the small port of Decamas,
and replenishing our wood and water, on the 2d October we set sail for the Galapagos Islands. We came
to anchor, and laid seven days off Hood Island, one
of the group; during which time we stopped a leak
which we had discovered, and obtained three hundred
turtle. We then visited Charles Island, where we procured sixty more. These turtle are a most delicious
food, and average in weight generally about one hundred pounds, but many of them weigh upwards of
eight hundred. With these, ships usually supply themselves for a great length of time, and make a great
saving of other provisions. They neither eat nor
drink, nor are the least pains taken with them; they

are strewed over the deck, thrown under foot, or packed away in the hold, as it suits convenience. They will live upwards of a year without food or water, but soon die in a cold climate. We left Charles Island on the 23rd of October, and steered off to the westward, in search of whales. In latitude 1° 0′ S., longitude 118° W. on the 16th of November, in the afternoon, we lost a boat during our work in a shoal of whales. I was in the boat myself, with five others, and was standing in the fore part, with the harpoon in my hand, well braced, expecting every instant to catch sight of one of the shoal which we were in, that I might strike; but judge of my astonishment and dismay, at finding myself suddenly thrown up in the air, my companions scattered about me, and the boat fast filling with water. A whale had come up directly under her, and with one dash of his tail had stove her bottom in, and strewed us in every direction around her. We, however, with little difficulty, got safely on the wreck, and clung there until one of the other boats which had been engaged in the shoal came to our assistance, and took us off. Strange to tell, not a man was injured by this accident. Thus it happens very frequently in the whaling business, that boats are stove; oars, harpoons, and lines broken; ankles and wrists sprained; boats upset, and whole crews left for hours in the water, without any of these accidents extending to the loss of life. We are so much accustomed to the continual recurrence of such scenes as these, that we become familiarized to them, and consequently always feel that confidence and self-possession, which teaches us every expedient in danger, and inures the body, as well as the mind, to fatigue, privation, and peril, in frequent cases exceeding belief. It is this danger and hardship that makes the sailor; indeed it is the distinguishing qualification amongst us; and it is a common boast of the whaleman that he has escaped from sudden and apparently inevitable destruction oftener than his fellow. He is accordingly valued on this account, without much reference to other qualities.

CHAPTER II.

I HAVE not been able to recur to the scenes which are now to become the subject of description, although a considerable time has elapsed, without feeling a mingled emotion of horror and astonishment at the almost incredible destiny that has preserved me and my surviving companions from a terrible death. Frequently, in my reflections on the subject, even after this lapse of time, I find myself shedding tears of gratitude for our deliverance, and blessing God, by whose divine aid and protection we were conducted through a series of unparalleled suffering and distress, and restored to the bosoms of our families and friends. There is no knowing what a stretch of pain and misery the human mind is capable of contemplating, when it is wrought upon by the anxieties of preservation; nor what pangs and weaknesses the body is able to endure, until they are visited upon it; and when at last deliverance comes, when the dream of hope is realized, unspeakable gratitude takes possession of the soul, and tears of joy choke the utterance. We require to be taught in the school of some signal suffering, privation, and despair, the great lessons of constant dependence upon an almighty forbearance and mercy. In the midst of the wide ocean, at night, when the sight of the heavens was shut out, and the dark tempest came upon us, then it was that we felt ourselves ready to exclaim, "Heaven have mercy upon us, for nought but that can save us now." But I proceed to the recital.—On the 20th of November (cruising in latitude 0° 40′ S., longitude 119° 0′ W.) , a shoal of whales was discovered off the lee-bow. The weather at this time was extremely fine and clear, and it was about 8 o'clock in the morning that the man at the mast-head gave the usual cry of, "There she blows." The ship was immediately put away, and we ran down in the direction for them. When we had got within half a mile of the place where they were observed, all our boats were lowered down, manned, and we started in pursuit of them. The ship, in the meantime, was brought to the wind, and the main-top-sail hove aback, to wait for us. I had the harpoon in the second boat; the captain preceded me in the first. When I arrived at the spot where we calculated they were, nothing was at first to be seen. We lay on our oars in anxious expectation of discovering them come up somewhere near us. Presently one rose, and spouted a short distance ahead of my boat; I made all speed towards it, came up with, and struck it; feeling the harpoon in him, he threw himself, in agony, over towards the boat (which at that time was up alongside of him) , and, giving a severe blow with his tail, struck the boat near the edge of the water, amidships, and stove a hole in her. I immediately took up the boat hatchet, and cut the line, to disengage the boat from the whale, which by this time was running off with great velocity. I succeeded in getting clear of him, with the loss of the harpoon and line; and finding the water to pour fast in the boat, I hastily stuffed three or four of our jackets in the hole, ordered one man to keep constantly bailing, and the rest to pull immediately for the ship; we succeeded in keeping the boat free, and shortly gained the ship. The captain and the second mate, in the other two boats, kept up the pursuit, and soon struck another whale. They being at this time a considerable distance to leeward, I went forward, braced around the mainyard, and put the ship off in a direction for them; the boat which had been stove was immediately hoisted in, and after examining the hole, I found that I could, by nailing a piece of canvas over it, get her ready to join in a fresh pursuit, sooner than by lowering down the other remaining boat which belonged to the ship. I accordingly turned her over upon the quarter, and was in the act of nailing on the canvas, when I observed a very large spermaceti whale, as well as I could judge about eighty-five feet in length; he broke water about twenty rods off our weather-bow, and was lying quietly, with his head in a direction for the ship. He spouted two or three times, and then disappeared. In less than two or three seconds he came up again, about the length of the ship off, and made directly for us, at the rate of about three knots. The ship was then going with about the same velocity. His appearance and attitude gave us at first no alarm; but while I stood watching his movements, and observing him but a ship's length off, coming down for us with great celerity, I involuntarily ordered the boy at the helm to put it hard up; intending to sheer off and avoid him. The words were scarcely out of my mouth, before he came down upon us with full speed, and struck the ship with his head, just forward of the fore-chains*;

* Between the platform where the foremast shrouds were secured and the bow of the ship.

he gave us such an appalling and tremendous jar, as nearly threw us all on our faces. The ship brought up as suddenly and violently as if she had struck a rock, and trembled for a few seconds like a leaf. We looked at each other with perfect amazement, deprived almost of the power of speech. Many minutes elapsed before we were able to realize the dreadful accident; during which time he passed under the ship, grazing her keel as he went along, came up alongside of her to leeward, and lay on the top of the water (apparently stunned with the violence of the blow) for the space of a minute; he then suddenly started off, in a direction to leeward. After a few moments reflection, and recovering, in some measure, from the sudden consternation that had seized us, I of course concluded that he had stove a hole in the ship, and that it would be necessary to set the pumps going. Accordingly they were rigged, but had not been in operation more than one minute before I perceived the head of the ship to be gradually settling down in the water; I then ordered the signal to be set for the other boats, which, scarcely had I despatched, before I again discovered the whale, apparently in convulsions, on the top of the water, about one hundred rods to leeward. He was enveloped in the foam of the sea, that his continual and violent thrashing about in the water had created around him, and I could distinctly see him smite his jaws together, as if distracted with rage and fury. He remained a short time in this situation, and then started off with great velocity, across the bows of the ship, to windward. By this time the ship had settled down a considerable distance in

the water, and I gave her up for lost. I, however, ordered the pumps to be kept constantly going, and
endeavoured to collect my thoughts for the occasion.
I turned to the boats, two of which we then had with
the ship, with an intention of clearing them away,
and getting all things ready to embark in them, if
there should be no other resource left; and while my
attention was thus engaged for a moment, I was
aroused with the cry of a man at the hatchway, "Here
he is—he is making for us again." I turned around,
and saw him about one hundred rods directly ahead
of us, coming down apparently with twice his ordinary speed, and to me at that moment, it appeared with
tenfold fury and vengeance in his aspect. The surf
flew in all directions about him, and his course towards us was marked by a white foam of a rod in
width, which he made with the continual violent
thrashing of his tail; his head was about half out of
water, and in that way he came upon, and again
struck the ship. I was in hopes when I descried him
making for us, that by a dexterous movement of putting the ship away immediately, I should be able to
cross the line of his approach, before he could get up
to us, and thus avoid what I knew, if he should strike
us again, would prove our inevitable destruction. I
bawled out to the helmsman, "Hard up!" but she
had not fallen off more than a point, before we took
the second shock. I should judge the speed of the ship
to have been at this time about three knots, and that
of the whale about six. He struck her to windward,
directly under the cathead,* and completely stove in

* A projecting timber near the bow, to which the anchor is
hoisted.

her bows. He passed under the ship again, went off to leeward, and we saw no more of him. Our situation at this juncture can be more readily imagined than described. The shock to our feelings was such, as I am sure none can have an adequate conception of that were not there: the misfortune befell us at a moment when we least dreamt of any accident; and from the pleasing anticipations we had formed, of realizing the certain profits of our labour, we were dejected by a sudden, most mysterious, and overwhelming calamity. Not a moment, however, was to be lost in endeavouring to provide for the extremity to which it was now certain we were reduced. We were more than a thousand miles from the nearest land, and with nothing but a light open boat, as the resource of safety for myself and companions. I ordered the men to cease pumping, and every one to provide for himself; seizing a hatchet at the same time, I cut away the lashings of the spare boat, which lay bottom up across two spars directly over the quarter deck, and cried out to those near me to take her as she came down. They did so accordingly, and bore her on their shoulders as far as the waist of the ship. The steward had in the meantime gone down into the cabin twice, and saved two quadrants, two practical navigators*, and the captain's trunk and mine; all which were hastily thrown into the boat, as she lay on the deck, with the two compasses which I snatched from the binnacle.† He attempted to descend again; but the water by this

---

* Probably Nathaniel Bowditch's *New American Practical Navigator;* the fourth edition was issued in 1817.
† A non-magnetic stand for the compass.

time had rushed in, and he returned without being able to effect his purpose. By the time we had got the boat to the waist, the ship had filled with water, and was going down on her beam-ends: we shoved our boat as quickly as possible from the plank-shear* into the water, all hands jumping in her at the same time, and launched off clear of the ship. We were scarcely two boat lengths distant from her, when she fell over to windward, and settled down in the water.

Amazement and despair now wholly took possession of us. We contemplated the frightful situation the ship lay in, and thought with horror upon the sudden and dreadful calamity that had overtaken us. We looked upon each other, as if to gather some consolatory sensation from an interchange of sentiments, but every countenance was marked with the paleness of despair. Not a word was spoken for several minutes by any of us; all appeared to be bound in a spell of stupid consternation; and from the time we were first attacked by the whale, to the period of the fall of the ship, and of our leaving her in the boat, more than ten minutes could not certainly have elapsed! God only knows in what way, or by what means, we were enabled to accomplish in that short time what we did; the cutting away and transporting the boat from where she was deposited would of itself, in ordinary circumstances, have consumed as much time as that, if the whole ship's crew had been employed in it. My companions had not saved a single article but what they had on their backs; but to me it was a source of infinite satisfaction, if any such

* A timber around a vessel's hull at deck line.

could be gathered from the horrors of our gloomy
situation, that we had been fortunate enough to have
preserved our compasses, navigators, and quadrants.
After the first shock of my feelings was over, I enthusi-
astically contemplated them as the probable instruments of our salvation; without them all would have
been dark and hopeless. Gracious God! what a picture of distress and suffering now presented itself to
my imagination. The crew of the ship were saved,
consisting of twenty human souls. All that remained
to conduct these twenty beings through the stormy
terrors of the ocean, perhaps many thousand miles,
were three open light boats. The prospect of obtaining any provisions or water from the ship, to subsist
upon during the time, was at least now doubtful.
How many long and watchful nights, thought I, are
to be passed? How many tedious days of partial starvation are to be endured, before the least relief or
mitigation of our sufferings can be reasonably anticipated. We lay at this time in our boat, about two
ship lengths off from the wreck, in perfect silence,
calmly contemplating her situation, and absorbed in
our own melancholy reflections, when the other boats
were discovered rowing up to us. They had but shortly before discovered that some accident had befallen
us, but of the nature of which they were entirely ignorant. The sudden and mysterious disappearance
of the ship was first discovered by the boat-steerer in
the captain's boat, and with a horror-struck countenance and voice, he suddenly exclaimed, "Oh, my God!
where is the ship?" Their operations upon this were instantly suspended, and a general cry of horror and de-

spair burst from the lips of every man, as their looks
were directed for her, in vain, over every part of the
ocean. They immediately made all haste towards us.
The captain's boat was the first that reached us. He
stopped about a boat's length off, but had no power to
utter a single syllable: he was so completely overpowered with the spectacle before him that he sat down
in his boat, pale and speechless. I could scarcely rec-
ognise his countenance, he appeared to be so much
altered, awed, and overcome with the oppression of
his feelings, and the dreadful reality that lay before
him. He was in a short time however enabled to address the inquiry to me, "My God, Mr. Chase, what
is the matter?" I answered, "We have been stove by a
whale." I then briefly told him the story. After a few
moment's reflection he observed that we must cut
away her masts, and endeavour to get something out
of her to eat. Our thoughts were now all accordingly
bent on endeavours to save from the wreck whatever
we might possibly want, and for this purpose we
rowed up and got on to her. Search was made for
every means of gaining access to her hold; and for
this purpose the lanyards were cut loose, and with
our hatchets we commenced to cut away the masts,
that she might right up again, and enable us to scut-
tle her decks. In doing which we were occupied
about three quarters of an hour, owing to our having
no axes, nor indeed any other instruments, but the
small hatchets belonging to the boats. After her masts
were gone she came up about two-thirds of the way
upon an even keel. While we were employed about
the masts the captain took his quadrant, shoved off

from the ship, and got an observation. We found
ourselves in latitude 0° 40' S., longitude 119° W. We
now commenced to cut a hole through the planks, directly above two large casks of bread, which most
fortunately were between decks, in the waist of the
ship, and which being in the upper side, when she
upset, we had strong hopes was not wet. It turned
out according to our wishes, and from these casks we
obtained six hundred pounds of hard bread. Other
parts of the deck were then scuttled, and we got without difficulty as much fresh water as we dared to take
in the boats, so that each was supplied with about
sixty-five gallons; we got also from one of the lockers
a musket, a small canister of powder, a couple of files,
two rasps, about two pounds of boat nails, and a few
turtles. In the afternoon the wind came on to blow a
strong breeze; and having obtained every thing that
occurred to us could then be got out, we began to
make arrangements for our safety during the night.
A boat's line was made fast to the ship, and to the
other end of it one of the boats was moored, at about
fifty fathoms to leeward; another boat was then at-
tached to the first one, about eight fathoms astern;
and the third boat, the like distance astern of her.
Night came on just as we had finished our operations;
and such a night as it was to us! so full of feverish
and distracting inquietude, that we were deprived
entirely of rest. The wreck was constantly before my
eyes. I could not, by any effort, chase away the horrors of the preceding day from my mind: they haunted me the live-long night. My companions—some of
them were like sick women; they had no idea of the

extent of their deplorable situation. One or two slept unconcernedly, while others wasted the night in unavailing murmurs. I now had full leisure to examine, with some degree of coolness, the dreadful. circumstances of our disaster. The scenes of yesterday passed in such quick succession in my mind that it was not until after many hours of severe reflection that I was able to discard the idea of the catastrophe as a dream. Alas! it was one from which there was no awaking; it was too certainly true, that but yesterday we had existed as it were, and in one short moment had been cut off from all the hopes and prospects of the living! I have no language to paint out the horrors of our situation. To shed tears was indeed altogether unavailing, and withal unmanly; yet I was not able to deny myself the relief they served to afford me. After several hours of idle sorrow and repining I began to reflect upon the accident, and endeavoured to realize by what unaccountable destiny or design (which I could not at first determine) this sudden and most deadly attack had been made upon us: by an animal, too, never before suspected of premeditated violence, and proverbial for its insensibility and inoffensiveness. Every fact seemed to warrant me in concluding that it was anything but chance which directed his operations; he made two several attacks upon the ship, at a short interval between them, both of which, according to their direction, were calculated to do us the most injury, by being made ahead, and thereby combining the speed of the two objects for the shock; to effect which, the exact manoeuvres which he made were necessary. His aspect was

most horrible, and such as indicated resentment and
fury. He came directly from the shoal which we had
just before entered, and in which we had struck three
of his companions, as if fired with revenge for their
sufferings. But to this it may be observed, that the
mode of fighting which they always adopt is either
with repeated strokes of their tails, or snapping of
their jaws together; and that a case, precisely similar
to this one, has never been heard of amongst the old-
est and most experienced whalers. To this I would
answer, that the structure and strength of the whale's
head is admirably designed for this mode of attack;
the most prominent part of which is almost as hard
and as tough as iron; indeed, I can compare it to
nothing else but the inside of a horse's hoof, upon
which a lance or harpoon would not make the slight-
est impression. The eyes and ears are removed nearly
one-third the length of the whole fish, from the front
part of the head, and are not in the least degree en-
dangered in this mode of attack. At all events, the
whole circumstances taken together, all happening
before my own eyes, and producing, at the time, impressions in my mind of decided, calculating mischief
on the part of the whale (many of which impressions
I cannot now recall) induce me to be satisfied that I
am correct in my opinion. It is certainly, in all its
bearings, a hitherto unheard of circumstance, and
constitutes, perhaps, the most extraordinary one in
the annals of the fishery.

CHAPTER III.

NOVEMBER 21st. The morning dawned upon our wretched company. The weather was fine, but the wind blew a strong breeze from the S.E. and the sea was very rugged. Watches had been kept up during the night, in our respective boats, to see that none of the spars or other articles (which continued to float out of the wreck) should be thrown by the surf against, and injure the boats. At sunrise, we began to think of doing something; what, we did not know: we cast loose our boats, and visited the wreck, to see if anything more of consequence could be preserved, but everything looked cheerless and desolate, and we made a long and vain search for any useful article; nothing could be found but a few turtle; of these we had enough already; or at least, as many as could be safely stowed in the boats, and we wandered around in every part of the ship in a sort of vacant idleness for the greater part of the morning. We were presently aroused to a perfect sense of our destitute and forlorn condition, by thoughts of the means which we had for our subsistence, the necessity of not wasting our time, and of endeavouring to seek some relief wherever God might direct us. Our thoughts, indeed, hung about the ship, wrecked and sunken as she was, and we could scarcely discard from our minds the idea of her continuing protection. Some great efforts in our situation were necessary, and a great deal of calculation important, as it concerned the means by which our existence was to be supported during, per-

haps, a very long period, and a provision for our
eventual deliverance. Accordingly, by agreement, all
set to work in stripping off the light sails of the ship,
for sails to our boats; and the day was consumed in
making them up and fitting them. We furnished
ourselves with masts and other light spars that were
necessary, from the wreck. Each boat was rigged with
two masts, to carry a flying-jib and two sprit-sails; the
sprit-sails were made so that two reefs could be taken
in them, in case of heavy blows. We continued to
watch the wreck for any serviceable articles that
might float from her, and kept one man during the
day, on the stump of her foremast, on the lookout
for vessels. Our work was very much impeded by the
increase of the wind and sea, and the surf breaking
almost continually into the boats gave us many fears
that we should not be able to prevent our provisions
from getting wet; and above all served to increase the
constant apprehensions that we had of the insufficien-
cy of the boats themselves during the rough weather
that we should necessarily experience. In order to
provide as much as possible against this, and withal
to strengthen the slight materials of which the boats
were constructed, we procured from the wreck some
light cedar boards (intended to repair boats in cases
of accidents) with which we built up additional
sides, about six inches above the gunwale; these, we
afterwards found, were of infinite service for the purpose for which they were intended; in truth, I am
satisfied we could never have been preserved without
them; the boats must otherwise have taken in so much
water that all the efforts of twenty such weak, starving

men as we afterwards came to be, would not have
sufficed to keep her free; but what appeared most immediately to concern us, and to command all our
anxieties, was the security of our provisions from the
salt water. We disposed of them under a covering of
wood, that whale-boats have at either end of them,
wrapping it up in several thicknesses of canvass. I
got an observation to-day, by which I found we were
in latitude 0° 6' S., longitude 119° 30' W., having been
driven by the winds a distance of forty-nine miles the
last twenty-four hours; by this it would appear that
there must have been a strong current, setting us to
the N.W. during the whole time. We were not able
to finish our sails in one day; and many little things
preparatory to taking a final leave of the ship were
necessary to be attended to, but evening came and put
an end to our labours. We made the same arrangements for mooring the boats in safety, and consigned
ourselves to the horrors of another tempestuous night.
The wind continued to blow hard, keeping up a heavy
sea, and veering around from S.E. to E. and E.S.E.
As the gloom of the night approached, and obliged
us to desist from that employment, which cheated us
out of some of the realities of our situation, we all of
us again became mute and desponding: a considerable degree of alacrity had been manifested by many
the preceding day, as their attention had been wholly
engaged in scrutinizing the wreck, and in construc-
ting the sails and spars for the boats; but when they
ceased to be occupied, they passed to a sudden fit of
melancholy, and the miseries of their situation came
upon them with such force, as to produce spells of

extreme debility, approaching almost to fainting. Our provisions were scarcely touched—the appetite was entirely gone; but as we had a great abundance of water, we indulged in frequent and copious draughts, which our parched mouths seemed continually to need. None asked for bread. Our continued state of anxiety during the night excluded all hopes of sleep; still (although the solemn fact had been before me for nearly two days) my mind manifested the utmost repugnance to be reconciled to it; I laid down in the bottom of the boat, and resigned myself to reflection; my silent prayers were offered up to the God of mercy, for that protection which we stood so much in need of. Sometimes, indeed, a light hope would dawn, but then, to feel such an utter dependence on and consignment to chance alone for aid and rescue, would chase it again from my mind. The wreck—the mysterious and mortal attack of the animal—the sudden prostration and sinking of the vessel—our escape from her, and our then forlorn and almost hapless destiny, all passed in quick and perplexing review in my imagination; wearied with the exertion of the body and mind, I caught, near morning, an hour's respite from my troubles, in sleep.

November 22nd. The wind remained the same, and the weather continued remarkably fine. At sunrise, we again hauled our boats up, and continued our search for articles that might float out. About 7 o'clock, the deck of the wreck began to give way, and every appearance indicated her speedy dissolution; the oil had bilged in the hold, and kept the surface of the sea all around us completely covered with it; the bulk-heads were all washed down, and she worked in every part of her joints and seams, with the violent and continual breaking of the surf over her. Seeing, at last, that little or nothing further could be done by remaining with the wreck, and as it was all-important that while our provisions lasted we should make the best possible use of time, I rowed up to the captain's boat, and asked him what he intended to do. I informed him that the ship's decks had bursted up, and that in all probability she would soon go to pieces; that no further purpose could be answered, by remaining longer with her, since nothing more could be obtained from her; and that it was my opinion no time should be lost in making the best of our way towards the nearest land. The captain observed, that he would go once more to the wreck, and survey her, and, after waiting until 12 o'clock for the purpose of getting an observation, would immediately after determine. In the meantime, before noon all our sails were completed, and the boats otherwise got in readiness for our departure. Our observation now proved us to be in latitude 0° 13' N., longitude 120° 00' W. as near as we could determine it, having crossed the equator during the night, and drifted nineteen miles. The wind had veered considerably to the eastward, during the last twenty-four hours. Our nautical calculations having been completed, the captain, after visiting the wreck, called a council, consisting of himself and the first and second mates, who all repaired to his boat, to interchange opinions and devise the best means for our security and preservation. There were, in all

of us, twenty men, six of whom were blacks, and we
had three boats. We examined our navigators, to
ascertain the nearest land, and found it was the Marquesas Islands. The Society Islands were next; these
islands we were entirely ignorant of; if inhabited, we
presumed they were by savages, from whom we had
as much to fear as from the elements, or even death
itself. We had no charts from which our calculations
might be aided, and were consequently obliged to
govern ourselves by the navigators alone; it was also
the captain's opinion that this was the season of the
hurricanes which prevail in the vicinity of the Sandwich Islands, and that consequently it would be un-
safe to steer for them. The issue of our deliberations
was that, taking all things into consideration, it
would be most advisable to shape our course by the
wind, to the southward, as far as 25° or 26° S. latitude, fall in with the variable winds, and then, endeavour to get eastward to the coast of Chili or Peru.
Accordingly, preparations were made for our immediate departure; the boat which it was my fortune,
or rather misfortune to have, was the worst of the
three, she was old and patched up, having been
stove a number of times during the cruise. At best,
a whale-boat is an extremely frail thing; the most so
of any other kind of boat; they are what is called
clinker built,* and constructed of the lightest materials, for the purpose of being rowed with the
greatest possible celerity according to the necessities
of the business for which they are intended. Of all
species of vessels, they are the weakest, and most fra-

* Built with overlapping boards.

gile, and possess but one advantage over any other—
that of lightness and buoyancy, that enables them to
keep above the dash of the sea with more facility than
heavier ones. This qualification is, however, preferable to that of any other, and, situated as we then
were, I would not have exchanged her, old and crazy
as she was, for even a ship's launch. I am quite confident that to this quality of our boats we most especially owed our preservation through the many
days and nights of heavy weather that we afterwards
encountered. In consideration of my having the weakest boat, six men were allotted to it; while those of
the captain and second mate, took seven each, and
at half past 12 we left the wreck, steering our course,
with nearly all sail set, S.S.E. At four o'clock in the
afternoon we lost sight of her entirely. Many were
the lingering and sorrowful looks we cast behind us.

It has appeared to me often since to have been, in
the abstract, an extreme weakness and folly, on our
parts, to have looked upon our shattered and sunken
vessel with such an excessive fondness and regret; but
it seemed as if in abandoning her we had parted with
all hope, and were bending our course away from her,
rather by some dictate of despair. We agreed to keep
together, in our boats, as nearly as possible to afford
assistance in case of accident, and to render our reflections less melancholy by each other's presence. I
found it on this occasion true, that misery does indeed love company; unaided, and unencouraged by
each other, there were with us many whose weak
minds, I am confident, would have sunk under the
dismal retrospections of the past catastrophe, and who

did not possess either sense or firmness enough to contemplate our approaching destiny without the cheering of some more determined countenance than their own. The wind was strong all day; and the sea ran very high, our boat taking in water from her leaks continually, so that we were obliged to keep one man constantly bailing. During the night the weather became extremely rugged, and the sea every now and then broke over us. By agreement, we were divided into two watches; one of which was to be constantly awake, and doing the labors of the boat, such as bailing, setting, taking in, and trimming the sails. We kept our course very well together during this night, and had many opportunities of conversation with the men in the other boats, wherein the means and prospects of our deliverance were variously considered; it appeared from the opinions of all that we had most to hope for in the meeting with some vessel, and most probably some whale ship, the great majority of whom, in those seas, we imagined were cruising about the latitude we were then steering for; but this was only a hope, the realization of which did not in any degree depend on our own exertions, but on chance alone. It was not, therefore, considered prudent, by going out of our course with the prospect of meeting them, to lose sight for one moment of the strong probabilities which, under Divine Providence, there were of our reaching land by the route we had prescribed to ourselves; as that depended, most especially, on a reasonable calculation, and on our own labors, we conceived that our provision and water, on a small allowance, would last us sixty days; that with the trade wind, on the course we were then lying, we should be able to average the distance of a degree a day, which, in 26 days, would enable us to attain the region of the variable winds, and then, in thirty more, at the very utmost, should there be any favor in the elements, we might reach the coast. With these considerations we commenced our voyage; the total failure of all which, and the subsequent dismal distress and suffering, by which we were overtaken, will be shown in the sequel. Our allowance of provision at first consisted of bread, one biscuit, weighing about one pound three ounces, and half a pint of water a day, for each man. This small quantity (less than one third which is required by an ordinary person), small as it was, we however took without murmuring, and, on many occasions afterwards, blest God that even this pittance was allowed to us in our misery. The darkness of another night overtook us; and after having for the first time partook of our allowance of bread and water, we laid our weary bodies down in the boat, and endeavoured to get some repose. Nature became at last worn out with the watchings and anxieties of the two preceding nights, and sleep came insensibly upon us. No dreams could break the strong fastenings of forgetfulness in which the mind was then locked up; but for my own part, my thoughts so haunted me that this luxury was yet a stranger to my eyes; every recollection was still fresh before me, and I enjoyed but a few short and unsatisfactory slumbers caught in the intervals between my hopes and my fears. The dark ocean and swelling waters were nothing; the fears of being swallowed up by some dreadful tempest,

or dashed upon hidden rocks, with all the other ordinary subjects of fearful contemplation, seemed
scarcely entitled to a moment's thought; the dismal
looking wreck, and the horrid aspect and revenge of
the whale, wholly engrossed my reflections, until day
again made its appearance.

November 23rd. In my chest, which I was fortunate
enough to preserve, I had several small articles which
we found of great service to us; among the rest, some
eight or ten sheets of writing paper, a lead pencil, a
suit of clothes, three small fish hooks, a jack-knife, a
whetstone, and a cake of soap. I commenced to keep
a sort of journal with the little paper and pencil
which I had; and the knife, besides other useful pur-
poses, served us as a razor. It was with much difficulty, however, that I could keep any sort of record,
owing to the incessant rocking and unsteadiness of
the boat, and the continual dashing of the spray of
the sea over us. The boat contained, in addition to
the articles enumerated, a lantern, tinder-box, and
two or three candles, which belonged to her, and with
which they are kept always supplied while engaged in
taking whale. In addition to all which, the captain
had saved a musket, two pistols, and a canister, con-
taining about two pounds of gunpowder; the latter he
distributed in equal proportions between the three
boats, and gave the second mate and myself each a
pistol. When morning came we found ourselves quite
near together, and the wind had considerably increased since the day before; we were consequently
obliged to reef our sails; and although we did not
apprehend any very great danger from the then vio-

lence of the wind, yet it grew to be very uncomfort-
able in the boats from the repeated dashing of the
waves that kept our bodies constantly wet with the
salt spray. We, however, stood along our course until
twelve o'clock, when we got an observation, as well as
we were able to obtain one, while the water flew all
over us, and the sea kept the boat extremely unsteady.
We found ourselves this day in latitude 0° 58′ S. having repassed the equator. We abandoned the idea
altogether of keeping any correct longitudinal reck-
oning, having no glass, nor log-line. The wind mod-
erated in the course of the afternoon a little, but at
night came on to blow again almost a gale. We began
now to tremble for our little barque; she was so ill
calculated, in point of strength, to withstand the racking of the sea, while it required the constant labors
of one man to keep her free of water. We were surrounded in the afternoon with porpoises that kept
playing about us in great numbers, and continued to
follow us during the night.

November 24th. The wind had not abated any
since the preceding day, and the sea had risen to be
very large, and increased, if possible, the extreme uncomfortableness of our situation. What added more
than anything else to our misfortunes was that all our
efforts for the preservation of our provisions proved,
in a great measure, ineffectual; a heavy sea broke suddenly into the boat, and, before we could snatch it
up, damaged some part of it; by timely attention, however, and great caution, we managed to make it eat-
able and to preserve the rest from a similar casualty.
This was a subject of extreme anxiety to us; the ex-

pectation, poor enough of itself indeed, upon which our final rescue was founded, must change at once to hopelessness, deprived of our provisions, the only means of continuing us in the exercise, not only of our manual powers, but in those of reason itself; hence, above all other things, this was the object of our utmost solicitude and pains.

We ascertained, the next day, that some of the provisions in the captain's boat had shared a similar fate during the night; both which accidents served to arouse us to a still stronger sense of our slender reliance upon the human means at our command, and to show us our utter dependence on that divine aid which we so much the more stood in need of.

November 25th. No change of wind had yet taken place, and we experienced the last night the same wet and disagreeable weather of the preceding one. About eight o'clock in the morning we discovered that the water began to come fast in our boat, and in a few minutes the quantity increased to such a degree as to alarm us considerably for our safety; we commenced immediately a strict search in every part of her to discover the leak, and, after tearing up the ceiling or floor of the boat near the bows, we found it proceeded from one of the streaks or outside boards having bursted off there; no time was to be lost in devising some means to repair it. The great difficulty consisted in its being in the bottom of the boat, about six inches from the surface of the water; it was necessary, therefore, to have access to the outside, to enable us to fasten it on again: the leak being to leeward, we hove about, and lay to on the other tack, which brought it then nearly out of water; the captain, who was at the time ahead of us, seeing us manoeuvring to get the boat about, shortened sail, and presently tacked, and ran down to us. I informed him of our situation, and he came immediately alongside to our assistance. After directing all the men in the boat to get on one side, the other, by that means, heeled out of the water a considerable distance, and, with a little difficulty, we then managed to drive in a few nails, and secured it, much beyond our expectations. Fears of no ordinary kind were excited by this seemingly small accident. When it is recollected to what a slight vessel we had committed ourselves; our means of safety alone consisting in her capacity and endurance for many weeks, in all probability, yet to come, it will not be considered strange that this little accident should not only have damped our spirits considerably, but have thrown a great gloominess over the natural prospects of our deliverance. On this occasion, too, were we enabled to rescue ourselves from inevitable destruction by the possession of a few nails, without which (had it not been our fortune to save some from the wreck) we would, in all human calculations, have been lost: we were still liable to a recurrence of the same accident, perhaps to a still worse one, as, in the heavy and repeated racking of the swell, the progress of our voyage would serve but to increase the incapacity and weakness of our boat, and the starting of a single nail in her bottom would most assuredly prove our certain destruction. We wanted not this additional reflection, to add to the miseries of our situation.

November 26th. Our sufferings, heaven knows, were now sufficiently increased, and we looked forward, not without an extreme dread, and anxiety, to the gloomy and disheartening prospect before us. We experienced a little abatement of wind and rough weather today, and took the opportunity of drying the bread that had been wet the day previously; to our great joy and satisfaction also, the wind hauled out to E.N.E. and enabled us to hold a much more favorable course; with these exceptions, no circumstance of any considerable interest occurred in the course of this day.

The 27th of November was alike undistinguished for any incident worthy of note; except that the wind again veered back to E. and destroyed the fine prospect we had entertained of making a good run for several days to come.

November 28th. The wind hauled still further to the southward, and obliged us to fall off our course to S. and commenced to blow with such violence, as to put us again under short sail; the night set in extremely dark, and tempestuous, and we began to entertain fears that we should be separated. We however, with great pains, managed to keep about a ship's length apart, so that the white sails of our boats could be distinctly discernible. The captain's boat was but a short distance astern of mine, and that of the second mate a few rods to leeward of his. At about 11 o'clock at night, having laid down to sleep, in the bottom of the boat, I was suddenly awakened by one of my companions, who cried out that the captain was in distress and was calling on us for assis-

tance. I immediately aroused myself, and listened a
moment, to hear if anything further should be said,
when the captain's loud voice arrested my attention.
He was calling to the second mate, whose boat was
nearer to him than mine. I made all haste to put
about, ran down to him, and inquired what was the
matter; he replied, "I have been attacked by an unknown fish, and he has stove my boat." It appeared
that some large fish had accompanied the boat for
a short distance, and had suddenly made an unpro-
voked attack upon her, as nearly as they could determine, with his jaws; the extreme darkness of the
night prevented them from distinguishing what kind
of animal it was, but they judged it to be about
twelve feet in length, and one of the killer-fish species. After having struck the boat once, he continued
to play about her, on every side, as if manifesting
a disposition to renew the attack, and did a second
time strike the bows of the boat, and split her stem.
They had no other instrument of violence but the
sprit-pole (a long slender piece of wood, by which
the peak of the sail is extended) with which, after
repeated attempts to destroy the boat, they succeeded in beating him off. I arrived just as he had dis-
continued his operations and disappeared. He had
made a considerable breach in the bows of the boat,
through which the water had began to pour fast; and
the captain, imagining matters to be considerably
worse then they were, immediately took measures to
remove his provisions into the second mate's boat
and mine, in order to lighten his own, and by that
means, and constant bailing, to keep her above wa-

ter until daylight should enable him to discover the extent of the damage, and to repair it. The night was spissy* darkness itself; the sky was completely overcast, and it seemed to us as if fate was wholly relentless, in pursuing us with such a cruel complication of disasters. We were not without our fears that the fish might renew his attack some time during the night upon one of the other boats, and unexpectedly destroy us; but they proved entirely groundless, as he was never afterwards seen. When daylight came, the wind again favoured us a little, and we all lay to, to repair the broken boat; which was effected by nailing on thin strips of boards in the inside; and, having replaced the provisions, we proceeded again on our course. Our allowance of water, which in the commencement merely served to administer to the positive demands of nature, became now to be insufficient; and we began to experience violent thirst from the consumption of the provisions that had been wet with the salt water, and dried in the sun; of these we were obliged to eat first, to prevent their spoiling; and we could not, nay, we did not dare, to make any encroachments on our stock of water. Our determination was to suffer as long as human patience and endurance would hold out, having only in view the relief that would be afforded us when the quantity of wet provisions should be exhausted. Our extreme sufferings here first commenced. The privation of water is justly ranked among the most dreadful of the miseries of our life; the violence of raving thirst has no parallel in the

* Dense.

catalogue of human calamities. It was our hard lot
to have felt this in its extremest force, when necessity subsequently compelled us to seek resource from
one of the offices of nature. We were not at first,
aware of the consequences of eating this bread; and
themselves to a degree of oppression that we could
divine the cause of our extreme thirst. But, alas!
it was not until the fatal effects of it had shown
there was no relief. Ignorant, or instructed of the
fact, it was alike immaterial; it composed a part of
our subsistence, and reason imposed upon us the
necessity of its immediate consumption, as otherwise
it would have been lost to us entirely.

November 29th. Our boats appeared to be growing daily more frail and insufficient; the continual
flowing of the water into them seemed increased,
without our being able to assign it to any thing else
than a general weakness, arising from causes that
must in a short time, without some remedy or relief,
produce their total failure. We did not neglect,
however, to patch up and mend them, according to
our means, whenever we could discover a broken or
weak part. We this day found ourselves surrounded
by a shoal of dolphins; some, or one of which, we
tried in vain a long time to take. We made a small
line from some rigging that was in the boat, fastened
on one of the fish-hooks, and tied to it a small piece
of white rag; they took not the least notice of it, but
continued playing around us, nearly all day, mock-
ing both our miseries and our efforts.

November 30th. This was a remarkably fine day;
the weather not exceeded by any that we had ex-

perienced since we left the wreck. At one o'clock, I
proposed to our boat's crew to kill one of the turtle;
two of which we had in our possession. I need not say
that the proposition was hailed with the utmost en-
thusiasm; hunger had set its ravenous gnawings upon
our stomachs, and we waited with impatience to
suck the warm flowing blood of the animal. A small
fire was kindled in the shell of the turtle, and after
dividing the blood (of which there was about a gill)
among those of us who felt disposed to drink it, we
cooked the remainder, entrails and all, and enjoyed
from it an unspeakably fine repast. The stomachs
of two or three revolted at the sight of the blood, and
refused to partake of it; not even the outrageous
thirst that was upon them could induce them to
taste it; for myself, I took it like a medicine, to relieve the extreme dryness of my palate, and stopped
not to inquire whether it was anything else than a
liquid. After this, I may say exquisite banquet, our
bodies were considerably recruited, and I felt my
spirits now much higher than they had been at any
time before. By observation, this day we found ourselves in latitude 7° 53′ S., our distance from the
wreck, as nearly as we could calculate, was then about
four hundred and eighty miles.

December 1st. From the 1st to the 3rd of December, exclusive, there was nothing transpired of any
moment. Our boats as yet kept admirably well together, and the weather was distinguished for its
mildness and salubrity. We gathered consolation too
from a favourable slant which the wind took to N.E.
and our situation was not at that moment, we

thought, so comfortless as we had been led at first to
consider it; but, in our extravagant felicitations upon the blessing of the wind and weather, we forgot
our leaks, our weak boats, our own debility, our immense distance from land, the smallness of our stock
of provisions; all which, when brought to mind, with
the force which they deserved, were too well calculated to dishearten us, and cause us to sigh for the
hardships of our lot. Up to the 3rd of December,
the raging thirst of our mouths had not been but in
a small degree alleviated; had it not been for the
pains which that gave us, we should have tasted,
during this spell of fine weather, a species of enjoy-
ment, derived from a momentous forgetfulness of
our actual situation.

December 3rd. With great joy we hailed the last
crumb of our damaged bread, and commenced this
day to take our allowance of healthy provisions. The
salutary and agreeable effects of this change was felt
at first in so slight a degree as to give us no great satisfaction; but gradually, as we partook of our small
allowance of water, the moisture began to collect in
our mouths, and the parching fever of the palate im-
perceptibly left it. An accident here happened to us
which gave us a great momentary spell of uneasiness.
The night was dark, and the sky was completely
overcast, so that we could scarcely discern each other's
boats, when at about ten o'clock, that of the second
mate was suddenly missing. I felt for a moment
considerable alarm at her unexpected disappearance;
but after a little reflection I immediately hove to,
struck a light as expeditiously as possible, and hoist-

ed it at the masthead, in a lantern. Our eyes were now directed over every part of the ocean, in search of her, when, to our great joy, we discerned an answering light, about a quarter of a mile to leeward of us; we ran down to it, and it proved to be the lost boat. Strange as the extraordinary interest which we felt in each other's company may appear, and much as our repugnance to separation may seem to imply of weakness, it was the subject of our continual hopes and fears. It is truly remarked that misfortune more than anything else serves to endear us to our companions. So strongly was this sentiment engrafted upon our feelings, and so closely were the destinies of all of us involuntarily linked together, that, had one of the boats been wrecked and wholly lost, with all her provisions and water, we should have felt ourselves constrained, by every tie of humanity, to have taken the surviving sufferers into the other boats, and shared our bread and water with them, while a crumb of one or a drop of the other remained. Hard, indeed, would the case have been for all, and much as I have since reflected on the subject, I have not been able to realize, had it so happened, that a sense of our necessities would have allowed us to give so magnanimous and devoted a character to our feelings. I can only speak of the impressions which I recollect I had at the time. Subsequently, however, as our situation became more straightened and desperate, our conversation on this subject took a different turn; and it appeared to be an universal sentiment that such a course of conduct was calculated to weaken the chances of a final deliverance for some, and might be the only means of consigning every soul of us to a horrid death of starvation. There is no question but that an immediate separation, therefore, was the most politic measure that could be adopted, and that every boat should take its own separate chance: while we remained together, should any accident happen of the nature alluded to, no other course could be adopted than that of taking the survivors into the other boats, and giving up voluntarily what we were satisfied could alone prolong our hopes and multiply the chances of our safety, or unconcernedly witness their struggles in death, perhaps beat them from our boats, with weapons, back into the ocean. The expectation of reaching the land was founded upon a reasonable calculation of the distance, the means, and the subsistence; all which were scanty enough, God knows, and ill adapted to the probable exigencies of the voyage. Any addition to our own demands, in this respect, would not only injure, but actually destroy the whole system which we had laid down, and reduce us to a slight hope, derived either from the speedy death of some of our crew, or the falling in with some vessel. With all this, however, there was a desperate instinct that bound us together; we could not reason on the subject with any degree of satisfaction to our minds, yet we continued to cling to each other with a strong and involuntary impulse. This, indeed, was a matter of no small difficulty, and it constituted, more than anything else, a source of continual watching and inquietude. We would but turn our eyes away for a few moments, during some dark nights, and presently one of the boats would be missing. There was no other remedy than to heave to immediately and set a light, by which the missing boat might be directed to us. These proceedings necessarily interfered very much with our speed, and consequently lessened our hopes; but we preferred to submit to it, while the consequences were not so immediately felt, rather than part with the consolation which each other's presence afforded. Nothing of importance took place on the 4th of December; and on the 5th, at night, owing to the extreme darkness, and a strong wind, I again separated from the other boats. Finding they were not to be seen in any direction, I loaded my pistol and fired it twice; soon after the second discharge they made their appearance a short distance to windward, and we joined company, and again kept on our course, in which we contÍnued without any remarkable occurrence through the 6th and 7th of December. The wind during this period blew very strong, and much more unfavorably. Our boats continued to leak, and to take in a good deal of water over the gunwales.

December 8th. In the afternoon of this day the wind set in E.S.E. and began to blow much harder than we had yet experienced it; by twelve o'clock at night it had increased to a perfect gale, with heavy showers of rain, and we now began, from these dreadful indications, to prepare ourselves for destruction. We continued to take in sail by degrees, as the tempest gradually increased, until at last we were obliged to take down our masts. At this juncture we gave up entirely to the mercy of the waves. The sea and rain had wet us to the skin, and we sat down, silently, and with sullen resignation, awaiting our fate. We made an effort to catch some fresh water by spreading one of the sails, but after having spent a long time, and obtained but a small quantity in a bucket, it proved to be quite as salty as that from the ocean: this we attributed to its having passed through the sail which had been so often wet by the sea, and upon which, after drying so frequently in the sun, concretions of salt had been formed. It was a dreadful night—cut off from any imaginary relief—nothing remained but to await the approaching issue with firmness and resignation. The appearance of the heavens was dark and dreary, and the blackness that was spread over the face of the waters dismal beyond description. The heavy squalls, that followed each other in quick succession, were preceded by sharp flashes of lightning, that appeared to wrap our little barge in flames. The sea rose to a fearful height, and every wave that came looked as if it must be the last that would be necessary for our destruction. To an overruling Providence alone must be attributed our salvation from the horrors of that terrible night. It can be accounted for in no other way: that a speck of substance, like that which we were, before the driving terrors of the tempest, could have been conducted safely through it. At twelve o'clock it began to abate a little in intervals of two or three minutes, during which we would venture to raise up our heads and look to windward. Our boat was completely unmanageable; without sails, mast, or rudder, and had been driven, in the course of the afternoon and night, we knew not whither, nor how far. When the gale had in some measure subsided we made efforts to get a little sail upon her, and put her head towards the course we had been steering. My companions had not slept any during the whole night, and were dispirited and broken down to such a degree as to appear to want some more powerful stimulus than the fears of death to enable them to do their duty. By great exertions, however, towards morning we again set a double-reefed mainsail and jib upon her, and began to make tolerable progress on the voyage. An unaccountable good fortune had kept the boats together during all the troubles of the night: and the sun rose and showed the disconsolate faces of our companions once more to each other.

December 9th. By twelve o'clock this day we were enabled to set all sail as usual; but there continued to be a very heavy sea running, which opened the seams of the boats, and increased the leaks to an alarming degree. There was, however, no remedy for this but continual bailing, which had now become to be an extremely irksome and laborious task. By observation we found ourselves in latitude 17° 40′ S. At eleven o'clock at night, the captain's boat was unexpectedly found to be missing. After the last accident of this kind we had agreed, if the same should again occur, that, in order to save our time, the other boats should not heave to, as usual, but continue on their course until morning, and thereby save the great detention that must arise from such repeated delays. We, however concluded on this occasion to make a small effort, which, if it did not immediately prove the means of restoring the lost boat, we would discontinue, and again make sail. Accordingly we hove to for an hour, during which time I fired my pistol twice, and obtaining no tidings of the boat, we stood on our course. When daylight appeared she was to leeward of us, about two miles; upon observing her we immediately ran down, and again joined company.

December 10th. I have omitted to notice the gradual advances which hunger and thirst for the last six days, had made upon us. As the time had lengthened since our departure from the wreck, and the allowance of provision, making the demands of the appetite daily more and more importunate, they had created in us an almost uncontrollable temptation to violate our resolution, and satisfy, for once, the hard yearnings of nature from our stock; but a little reflection served to convince us of the imprudence and unmanliness of the measure, and it was abandoned with a sort of melancholy effort of satisfaction. I had taken into custody, by common consent, all the provisions and water belonging to the boat, and was determined that no encroachments should be made upon it with my consent; nay, I felt myself bound, by every consideration of duty, by every dictate of sense, of prudence, and discretion, without which, in my situation, all other exertions would have been folly itself, to protect them, at the hazard of my life. For this purpose I locked up in my chest the whole quantity, and never, for a single moment, closed my eyes without placing some part of my person in contact with the chest; and having loaded my pistol, kept it constantly about me. I should not certainly have put any threats in execution as long as the most distant hopes of reconciliation existed; and was determined, in case the least refractory disposition should be manifested (a thing which I contemplated not unlikely to happen, with a set of starving wretches like ourselves) that I would immediately divide our substance into equal proportions, and give each man's share into his own keeping. Then, should any attempt be made upon mine, which I intended to mete out to myself according to exigencies, I was resolved to make the consequences of it fatal. There was, however, the most upright and obedient behaviour in this respect manifested by every man in the boat, and I never had the least opportunity of proving what my conduct would have been on such an occasion. While standing on our course this day we came across a small shoal of flying fish: four of which, in their efforts to avoid us, flew against the mainsail, and dropped into the boat; one having fell near me, I eagerly snatched up and devoured; the other three were immediately taken by the rest, and eaten alive. For the first time I, on this occasion, felt a disposition to laugh, upon witnessing the ludicrous and almost desperate efforts of my five companions, who each sought to get a fish. They were very small of the ĸind, and constituted but an extremely delicate mouthful, scales, wings, and all, for hungry stomachs like ours. From the eleventh to the thirteenth of December inclusive, our progress was very slow, owing to light winds and calms; and nothing transpired of any moment, except that on the eleventh we kill-ed the only remaining turtle, and enjoyed another luxuriant repast, that invigorated our bodies, and gave a fresh flow to our spirits. The weather was extremely hot, and we were exposed to the full force of a meridian sun, without any covering to shield us from its burning influence, or the least breath of air to cool its parching rays. On the thirteenth day of December we were blessed with a change of wind to the northward, that brought us a most welcome and unlooked for relief. We now, for the first time, actually felt what might be deemed a reasonable hope of our deliverance; and with hearts bounding with satisfaction, and bosoms swelling with joy, we made all sail to the eastward. We imagined we had run out of the tradewinds, and had got into the variables, and should, in all probability, reach the land many days sooner than we expected. But, alas! our anticipations were but a dream, from which we shortly experienced a cruel awaking. The wind gradually died away, and at night was succeeded by a perfect calm, more oppressive and disheartening to us from the bright prospects which had attended us during the day. The gloomy reflections that this hard fortune had given birth to were succeeded by others, of a no less cruel and discouraging nature, when we found the calm continue during the fourteenth, fifteenth, and sixteenth of December inclusive. The extreme oppression of the weather, the sudden and unexpected prostration of our hopes, and the consequent dejection of our spirits, set us again to thinking, and filled our souls with fearful and melancholy forebodings. In this state of affairs, seeing no alternative left us but to employ to the best advantage all human expedients in our power, I proposed, on the fourteenth, to reduce our allowance of provisions one half. No objections were made to this arrangement: all submitted, or seemed to do so, with an admirable fortitude and forebearance. The proportion which our stock of water bore to our bread was not large; and while the weather continued so oppressive, we did not think it advisable to diminish our scanty pittance; indeed, it would have been scarcely possible to have done so, with any regard to our necessities, as our thirst had become now incessantly more intolerable than hunger, and the quantity then allowed was barely sufficient to keep the mouth in a state of moisture for about one-third of the time. "Patience and long-suffering" was the constant language of our lips: and a determination, strong as the resolves of the soul could make it, to cling to existence as long as hope and breath remained to us. In vain was every expedient tried to relieve the raging fever of the throat by drinking salt water, and holding small quantities of it in the mouth, until, by that means, the thirst was increased to such a degree, as even to drive us to despairing, and vain relief from our own urine. Our sufferings during these calm days almost exceeded human belief. The hot rays of the sun beat down upon us to such a degree as to oblige us to hang over the gunwale of the boat, into the sea, to cool our weak and fainting bodies. This expedient afforded us, however, a grateful relief, and was productive of a discovery of infinite importance to us. No sooner had one of us got on the outside of the gunwale than he immediately observed the bottom of the boat to be covered with a species of small clam, which upon being tasted, proved a most delicious and agreeable food. This was no sooner announced to us than we commenced to tear them off and eat them, for a few minutes, like a set of gluttons; and, after having satisfied the immediate craving of the stomach, we gathered large quantities and laid them up in the boat; but hunger came upon us again in less than half an hour afterwards, within which time they had all disappeared. Upon attempting to get in again, we found ourselves so weak as to require each other's assistance; indeed, had it not been for three of our crew, who could not swim, and who did not, therefore, get overboard, I know not by what means we should have been able to have resumed our situations in the boat.

On the fifteenth our boat continued to take in water so fast from her leaks, and the weather proving so moderate, we concluded to search out the bad places, and endeavour to mend them as well as we should be able. After a considerable search, and, removing the ceiling near the bows, we found the principal opening was occasioned by the starting of a plank or streak in the bottom of the boat, next to the keel. To remedy this, it was now absolutely necessary to have access to the bottom. The means of doing which did not immediately occur to our minds. After a moment's reflection, however, one of the crew, Benjamin Lawrence, offered to tie a rope around his body, take a boat's hatchet in his hand, and thus go under the water, and hold the hatchet against a nail, to be driven through from the inside, for the purpose of clenching it. This was, accordingly, all effected, with some little trouble, and answered the purpose much beyond our expectations. Our latitude was this day 21° 42′ South. The oppression of the weather still continuing through the sixteenth, bore upon our health and spirits with an amazing force and severity. The most disagreeable excitements were produced by it, which, added to the disconsolate endurance of the calm, called loudly for some mitigating expedient,—some sort of relief to our prolonged sufferings. By our observations today we found, in addition to our other calamities, that we had been urged back from our progress, by the heave of the sea, a distance of ten miles; and were still without any prospect of wind. In this distressing posture of our affairs, the captain proposed that we should commence rowing, which, being seconded by all, we immediately concluded to take a double allowance of provision and water for the day, and row, during the cool of the nights, until we should get a breeze from some quarter or other. Accordingly, when night came, we commenced our laborious operations: we made but a very sorry progress. Hunger and thirst, and long inactivity, had so weakened us, that in three hours every man gave out, and we abandoned the further prosecution of the plan. With the sunrise the next morning, on the seventeenth, a light breeze sprung up from the S.E. and, although directly ahead, it was welcomed with almost frenzied feelings of gratitude and joy.

December 18th. The wind increased this day considerably, and by twelve o'clock blew a gale; veering from S.E. to E.S.E. Again we were compelled to take in all sail, and lie to for the principal part of the day. At night, however, it died away, and the next day, the nineteenth, proved very moderate and pleasant weather, and we again commenced to make a little progress.

December 20th. This was a day of great happiness and joy. After having experienced one of the most distressing nights in the whole catalogue of our sufferings, we awoke to a morning of comparative luxury and pleasure. About 7 o'clock, while we were sitting dispirited, silent, and dejected, in our boats, one of our companions suddenly and loudly called out, "There is land!" We were all aroused in an instant, as if electrified, and casting our eyes to leeward, there indeed, was the blessed vision before us, "as plain and palpable" as could be wished for. A new and extraordinary impluse now took possession of us. We shook off the lethargy of our senses, and seemed to take another, and a fresh existence. One or two of my companions, whose lagging spirits and worn out frames had begun to inspire them with an utter indifference to their fate, now immediately brightened up, and manifested a surprising alacrity and earnestness to gain, without delay, the much wished for shore. It appeared at first a low, white, beach, and lay like a basking paradise before our longing eyes. It was discovered nearly at the same time by the other boats, and a general burst of joy and congratuulation now passed between us. It is not within the scope of human calculation, by a mere

listener to the story, to divine what the feelings of
our hearts were on this occasion. Alternate expectation, fear, gratitude, surprise, and exultation, each
swayed our minds, and quickened our exertions. We
ran down for it, and at 11 o'clock, A.M., we were
within a quarter of a mile of the shore. It was an
island, to all appearance, as nearly as we could determine it, about six miles long and three broad;
with a very high, rugged shore, and surrounded by
rocks; the sides of the mountains were bare, but on
the tops it looked fresh and green with vegetation.
Upon examining our navigators, we found it was
Ducie's Island,* lying in latitude 24° 40′ S., longitude
124° 40′ W. A short moment sufficed for reflection,
and we made immediate arrangements to land. None
of us knew whether the island was inhabited or not,
nor what it afforded, if any thing; if inhabited, it
was uncertain whether by beasts or savages; and a
momentary suspense was created by the dangers
which might possibly arise by proceeding without
due preparation and care. Hunger and thirst, however, soon determined us, and having taken the musket and pistols, I, with three others, effected a landing upon some sunken rocks, and waded thence to
the shore. Upon arriving at the beach, it was necessary to take a little breath, and we laid down for a
few minutes to rest our weak bodies before we could
proceed. Let the reader judge, if he can, what must
have been our feelings now! Bereft of all comfortable
hopes of life, for the space of thirty days of terrible
suffering; our bodies wasted to mere skeletons, by

* Actually Henderson Island.

hunger and thirst, and death itself staring us in the face; to be suddenly and unexpectedly conducted to a rich banquet of food and drink, which subsequently we enjoyed for a few days, to our full satisfaction; and he will have but a faint idea of the happiness that here fell to our lot. We now, after a few minutes, separated, and went different directions in search of water; the want of which had been our principal privation, and called for immediate relief. I had not proceeded far in my excursion, before I discovered a fish, about a foot and a half in length, swimming along in the water close to the shore. I commenced an attack upon him with the breach of my gun, and struck him, I believe, once and he ran under a small rock, that lay near the shore, from whence I took him with the aid of my ramrod, and brought him up on the beach, and immediately fell to eating. My companions soon joined in the repast; and in less than ten minutes, the whole was consumed, bones, and skin, and scales, and all. With full stomachs, we imagined we could now attempt the mountains, where, if in any part of the island, we considered water would be most probably obtained. I accordingly clambered, with excessive labor, suffering, and pain, up amongst the bushes, roots, and underwood, of one of the crags, looking in all directions in vain, for every appearance of water that might present itself. There was no indication of the least moisture to be found, within the distance to which I had ascended, although my strength did not enable me to get higher than about 20 feet. I was sitting down at the height that I had attained, to

gather a little breath, and ruminating upon the fruit-
lessness of my search, and, the consequent evils and
continuation of suffering that it necessarily implied,
when I perceived that the tide had risen considerably
since our landing, and threatened to cut off our re-
treat to the rocks, by which alone we should be able
to regain our boats. I therefore determined to proceed again to the shore, and inform the captain and
the rest of our want of success in procuring water,
and consult upon the propriety of remaining at the
island any longer. I never for one moment lost sight
of the main chance, which I conceived we still had,
of either getting to the coast, or of meeting with
some vessel at sea; and felt that every minute's detention, without some equivalent object, was lessen-
ing thoses chances, by a consumption of the means
of our support. When I had got down, one of my
companions informed me, that he had found a place
in a rock some distance off, from which the water
exuded in small drops, at intervals of about five
minutes; that he had, by applying his lips to the rock,
obtained a few of them, which only served to whet
his appetite, and from which nothing like the least
satisfaction had proceeded. I immediately resolved
in my own mind, upon this information, to advise
remaining until morning, to endeavour to make a
more thorough search the next day, and with our
hatchets to pick away the rock which had been discovered, with the view of increasing, if possible, the
run of the water. We all repaired again to our boats,
and there found that the captain had the same impressions as to the propriety of our delay until morn-

ing. We therefore landed; and having hauled our boats up on the beach, laid down in them that night, free from all the anxieties of watching and labor, and amid all our sufferings, gave ourselves up to an unreserved forgetfulness and peace of mind, that seemed so well to accord with the pleasing anticipations that this day had brought forth. It was but a short space, however, until the morning broke upon us; and sense, and feeling, and gnawing hunger, and the raging fever of thirst then redoubled my wishes and efforts to explore the island again. We had obtained, that night, a few crabs, by traversing the shore a considerable distance, and a few very small fish; but waited until the next day, for the labors of which, we considered a night of refreshing and undisturbed repose would better qualify us.

December 21st. We had still reserved our common allowance, but it was entirely inadequate for the purpose of supplying the raging demands of the palate; and such an excessive and cruel thirst was created, as almost to deprive us of the power of speech. The lips became cracked and swollen, and a sort of glutinous saliva collected in the mouth, disagreeable to the taste, and intolerable beyond expression. Our bodies had wasted away to almost skin and bone, and possessed so little strength as often to require each other's assistance in performing some of its weakest functions. Relief, we now felt, must come soon, or nature would sink. The most perfect discipline was still maintained in respect to our provisions; and it now became our whole object, if we should not be able to replenish our subsistence from the island, to obtain, by some means or other, a sufficient refreshment to enable us to prosecute our voyage.

Our search for water accordingly again commenced with the morning; each of us took a different direction, and prosecuted the examination of every place where there was the least indication of it; the small leaves of the shrubbery, affording a temporary alleviation, by being chewed in the mouth, and but for the peculiarly bitter taste which those of the island possessed, would have been an extremely grateful substitute. In the course of our rambles too, along the sides of the mountain, we would now and then meet with tropic birds, of a beautiful figure and plumage, occupying small holes in the sides of it, from which we plucked them without the least difficulty. Upon our approaching them they made no attempts to fly, nor did they appear to notice us at all. These birds served us for a fine repast; numbers of which were caught in the course of the day, cooked by fires which we made on the shore, and eaten with the utmost avidity. We found also a plant, in taste not unlike the peppergrass, growing in considerable abundance in the crevices of the rocks, and which proved to us a very agreeable food, by being chewed with the meat of the birds. These, with birds' nests, some of them full of young, and others of eggs, a few of which we found in the course of the day, served us for food, and supplied the place of our bread; from the use of which, during our stay here, we had restricted ourselves. But water, the great object of all our anxieties and exertions, was no where to be found, and we began to despair of meeting with it on the island. Our state of extreme weakness, and many of us without shoes or any covering for the feet, prevented us from exploring any great distance; lest by some sudden faintness, or over exertion, we should not be able to return, and at night be exposed to attacks of wild beasts, which might inhabit the island, and be alike incapable of resistance, as beyond the reach of the feeble assistance that otherwise could be afforded to each. The whole day was thus consumed in picking up whatever had the least shape or quality of sustenance, and another night of misery was before us, to be passed without a drop of water to cool our parching tongues. In this state of affairs, we could not reconcile it to ourselves to remain at this place; a day, an hour, lost to us unnecessarily here, might cost us our preservation. A drop of the water that we then had in our possession might prove, in the last stages of our debility, the very cordial of life. I addressed the substance of these few reflections to the captain, who agreed with me in opinion, upon the necessity of taking some decisive steps in our present dilemma. After some considerable conversation on this subject, it was finally concluded to spend the succeeding day in the further search for water, and if none should be found, to quit the island the morning after.

December 22nd. We had been employed during the last night in various occupations, according to the feelings or the wants of the men; some continued to wander about the shore, and to short distances in the mountains, still seeking for food and water; others hung about the beach, near the edge of the sea, endeavouring to take the little fish that came about them. Some slept, insensible to every feeling but rest; while others spent the night in talking of their situation, and reasoning upon the probabilities of their deliverance. The dawn of day aroused us again to labor, and each of us pursued his own inclination, as to the course taken over the island after water. My principal hope was founded upon my success in picking the rocks where the moisture had been discovered the day before, and thither I hastened as soon as my strength would enable me to get there. It was about a quarter of a mile from what I may call our encampment; and with two men, who had accompanied me, I commenced my labors with a hatchet and an old chisel. The rock proved to be very soft, and in a very short time I had obtained a considerable hole, but, alas! without the least wished for effect. I watched it for some little time with great anxiety, hoping that, as I increased the depth of the hole, the water would presently flow; but all my hopes and efforts were unavailing, and at last I desisted from further labor, and sat down near it in utter despair. As I turned my eyes towards the beach I saw some of the men in the act of carrying a keg along from the boats, with, I thought, an extraordinary spirit and activity; and the idea suddenly darted across my mind that they had found water, and were taking a keg to fill it. I quitted my seat in a moment, made the best of my way towards them, with a palpitating heart, and before I came up with them, they gave me the cheering news that they had found a spring of water. I felt, at that moment, as if I could have fallen down and thanked God for this signal act of his mercy. The sensation that I experienced was indeed strange, and such as I shall never forget. At one instant I felt an almost choking excess of joy, and at the next I wanted the relief of a flood of tears. When I arrived at the spot, whither I had hastened as fast as my weak legs would carry me, I found my companions had all taken their fill, and with an extreme degree of forbearance I then satisfied myself, by drinking in small quantities, and at intervals of two or three minutes apart. Many had, notwithstanding the remonstrances of prudence, and, in some cases, force, laid down and thoughtlessly swallowed large quantities of it, until they could drink no more. The effect of this was, however, neither so sudden nor bad as we had imagined; it only served to make them a little stupid and indolent for the remainder of the day.

Upon examining the place from whence we had obtained this miraculous and unexpected succour, we were equally astonished and delighted with the discovery. It was on the shore, above which the sea flowed to the depth of near six feet; and we could procure the water, therefore, from it only when the tide was down. The crevice from which it rose was in a flat rock, large surfaces of which were spread around, and composed the face of the beach. We filled our two kegs before the tide rose, and went back again to our boats. The remainder of this day was spent in seeking for fish, crabs, birds, and anything else that fell in our way, that could contribute to satisfy our appetites; and we enjoyed, during that

night, a most comfortable and delicious sleep, unat-
tended with those violent cravings of hunger and
thirst, that had poisoned our slumbers for so many
previous ones. Since the discovery of the water, too,
we began to entertain different notions altogether
of our situation. There was no doubt we might here
depend upon a constant and ample supply of it as
long as we chose to remain, and, in all probability,
we could manage to obtain food, until the island
should be visited by some vessel, or time allowed to
devise other means of leaving it. Our boats would
still remain to us: a stay here might enable us to
mend, strengthen, and put them in more perfect
order for the sea, and get ourselves so far recruited
as to be able to endure, if necessary, a more protract-
ed voyage to the main land. I made a silent determination in my own mind that I would myself pursue
something like this plan, whatever might be the opinion of the rest; but I found no difference in the views
of any of us as to this matter. We, therefore, concluded to remain at least four or five days, within
which time it could be sufficiently known whether it
would be advisable to make any arrangements for a
more permanent abode.

December 23rd. At 11 o'clock, A. M., we again visited our spring: the tide had fallen to about a foot
below it, and we were able to procure, before it rose
again, about twenty gallons of water. It was at first
a little brackish, but soon became fresh, from the constant supply from the rock and the departure of the
sea. Our observations this morning tended to give us
every confidence in its quantity and quality, and we,

therefore, rested perfectly easy in our minds on the subject, and commenced to make further discoveries about the island. Each man sought for his own daily living, on whatsoever the mountains, the shore, or the sea, could furnish him with; and every day, during our stay there, the whole time was employed in roving about for food. We found, however, on the twenty-fourth, that we had picked up, on the island, every thing that could be got at, in the way of sustenance; and, much to our surprise, some of the men came in at night and complained of not having gotten sufficient during the day to satisfy the cravings of their stomachs. Every accessible part of the mountain, contiguous to us, or within the reach of our weak enterprise, was already ransacked, for birds' eggs and grass, and was rifled of all that they contained: so that we began to entertain serious apprehensions that we should not be able to live long here; at any rate, with the view of being prepared, as well as possible, should necessity at any time oblige us to quit it, we commenced, on the twenty-fourth, to repair our boats, and continued to work upon them all that and the succeeding day. We were enabled to do this, with much facility, by drawing them up and turning them over on the beach, working by spells of two or three hours at a time, and then leaving off to seek for food. We procured our water daily, when the tide would leave the shore: but on the evening of the twenty-fifth, found that a fruitless search for nourishment had not repaid us for the labors of a whole day. There was no one thing on the island upon which we could in the least degree rely, except

the peppergrass, and of that the supply was pre-
carious, and not much relished without some
other food. Our situation here, therefore, now became worse than it would have been in our boats on
the ocean; because, in the latter case, we should be
still making some progress towards the land, while
our provisions lasted, and the chance of falling in
with some vessel be considerably increased. It was
certain that we ought not to remain here unless upon
the strongest assurances in our own minds, of sufficient
sustenance, and that, too, in regular supplies, that
might be depended upon. After much conversation
amongst us on this subject, and again examining our
navigators, it was finally concluded to set sail for
Easter Island, which we found to be E.S.E. from us
in latitude 27° 9′ S., longitude 109° 35′ W. All we
knew of this island was that it existed as laid down
in the books; but of its extent, productions, or inhabitants, if any, we were entirely ignorant; at any
rate, it was nearer by eight hundred and fifty miles to
the coast, and could not be worse in its productions
than the one we were about leaving.

The twenty-sixth of December was wholly employed in preparations for our departure; our boats were
hauled down to the vicinity of the spring, and our
casks, and everything else that would contain it, filled
with water.

There had been considerable talk between three
of our companions about their remaining on this island, and taking their chance both for a living, and
an escape from it; and as the time drew near at
which we were to leave, they made up their minds

his own boat, he died very suddenly after his removal.
On the eleventh, at six o'clock in the morning, we
sewed him up in his clothes, tied a large stone to his
feet, and, having brought all the boats to, consigned
him in a solemn manner to the ocean. This man did
not die of absolute starvation, although his end was
no doubt very much hastened by his sufferings. He
had a weak and sickly constitution, and complained
of being unwell the whole voyage. It was an incident,
however, which threw a gloom over our feelings for
many days. In consequence of his death, one man
from the captain's boat was placed in that from which
he died, to supply his place, and we stood away
again on our course.

On the 12th of January we had the wind from the
N.W. which commenced in the morning, and came
on to blow before night a perfect gale. We were
obliged to take in all sail and run before the wind.
Flashes of lightning were quick and vivid, and the
rain came down in cataracts. As, however, the gale
blew us fairly on our course, and our speed being
great during the day, we derived, I may say, even
pleasure from the uncomfortableness and fury of the
storm. We were apprehensive that in the darkness
of this night we should be separated, and made arrangements, each boat to keep an E.S.E. course all
night. About eleven o'clock my boat being ahead a
short distance of the others, I turned my head back,
as I was in the habit of doing every minute, and

neither of the others were to be seen. It was blowing and raining at this time as if the heavens were separating, and I knew not hardly at the moment what to do. I hove my boat to the wind, and lay drifting about an hour, expecting every moment they would come up with me, but not seeing anything of them, I put away again, and stood on the course agreed upon, with strong hopes that daylight would enable me to discover them again. When the morning dawned, in vain did we look over every part of the ocean for our companions; they were gone! and we saw no more of them afterwards. It was folly to repine at the circumstance; it could neither be remedied, nor could sorrow secure their return; but it was impossible to prevent ourselves feeling all the poignancy and bitterness that characterizes the separation of men who have long suffered in each other's company, and whose interests and feelings fate had so closely linked together. By our observation, we separated in latitude 32° 16′ S., longitude 112° 20′ W. For many days after this accident, our progress was attended with dull and melancholy reflections. We had lost the cheering of each other's faces, that which strange as it is, we so much required in both our mental and bodily distresses. The 14th January proved another very squally and rainy day. We had now been nineteen days from the island, and had only made a distance of about 900 miles: necessity began to whisper us, that a still further reduction of our allowance must take place, or we must abandon altogether the hopes of reaching the land, and rely wholly on the chance of being taken up by a vessel.

But how to reduce the daily quantity of food, with any regard to life itself, was a question of the utmost consequence. Upon our first leaving the wreck, the demands of the stomach had been circumscribed to the smallest possible compass; and subsequently before reaching the island, a diminution had taken place of nearly one-half; and it was now, from a reasonable calculation, become necessary even to curtail that at least one-half; which must, in a short time, reduce us to mere skeletons again. We had a full allowance of water, but it only served to contribute to our debility; our bodies deriving but the scanty support which an ounce and a half of bread for each man afforded. It required a great effort to bring matters to this dreadful alternative, either to feed our bodies and our hopes a little longer, or in the agonies of hunger to seize upon and devour our provisions, and coolly await the approach of death.

We were as yet, just able to move about in our boats, and slowly perform the necessary labors appertaining to her; but we were fast wasting away with the relaxing effects of the water, and we daily almost perished under the torrid rays of a meridian sun; to escape which, we would lie down in the bottom of the boat, cover ourselves over with the sails, and abandon her to the mercy of the waves. Upon attempting to rise again, the blood would rush into the head, and an intoxicating blindness come over us, almost to occasion our suddenly falling down again. A slight interest was still kept up in our minds by the distant hopes of yet meeting with the other boats, but it was never realized. An accident

occurred at night, which gave me a great cause of uneasiness, and led me to an unpleasant rumination
upon the probable consequences of a repetition of
it. I had laid down in the boat without taking the
usual precaution of securing the lid of the provision
chest, as I was accustomed to do, when one of the
white men awoke me, and informed me that one of
the blacks had taken some bread from it. I felt at
the moment the highest indignation and resentment
at such conduct in any of our crew and immediately
took my pistol in my hand, and charged him if he
had taken any, to give it up without the least hesita-
tion, or I should instantly shoot him!—He became at
once very much alarmed, and trembling, confessed the
fact, pleading the hard necessity that urged him to it:
he appeared to be very penitent for his crime, and earnestly swore that he would never be guilty of it again.
I could not find it in my soul to extend towards him
the least severity on this account, however much,
according to the strict imposition which we felt upon ourselves, it might demand it. This was the first
infraction; and the security of our lives, our hopes
of redemption from our sufferings, loudly called for
a prompt and signal punishment; but every humane
feeling of nature plead in his behalf, and he was
permitted to escape, with the solemn injunction that
a repetition of the same offence would cost him his
life.

I had almost determined upon this occurrence to
divide our provisions, and give to each man his share
of the whole stock; and should have done so in the
height of my resentment had it not been for the re-

flection that some might, by imprudence, be tempted to go beyond the daily allowance, or consume it all at once, and bring on a premature weakness or starvation: this would of course disable them for the duties of the boat, and reduce our chances of safety and deliverance.

On the 15th of January, at night, a very large shark was observed swimming about us in a most ravenous manner, making attempts every now and then upon different parts of the boat, as if he would devour the very wood with hunger; he came several times and snapped at the steering oar, and even the stern-post. We tried in vain to stab him with a lance, but we were so weak as not to be able to make any impression upon his hard skin; he was so much larger than an ordinary one, and manifested such a fearless malignity, as to make us afraid of him; and our utmost efforts, which were at first directed to kill him for prey, became in the end self-defense. Baffled however in all his hungry attempts upon us, he shortly made off.

On the 16th of January, we were surrounded with porpoises in great numbers, that followed us nearly an hour, and which also defied all manoeuvres to catch them. The 17th and 18th proved to be calm; and the distresses of a cheerless prospect and a burning hot sun were again visited upon our devoted heads.

We began to think that Divine Providence had abandoned us at last; and it was but an unavailing effort to endeavour to prolong a now tedious existence. Horrible were the feelings that took possession of us!—The contemplation of a death of agony and torment, refined by the most dreadful and distressing reflections, absolutely prostrated both body and soul. There was not a hope now remaining to us but that which was derived from a sense of the mercies of our Creator. The night of the 18th was a despairing era in our sufferings; our minds were wrought up to the highest pitch of dread and apprehension for our fate, and all in them was dark, gloomy, and confused. About 8 o'clock, the terrible noise of whale spouts near us sounded in our ears: we could distinctly hear the furious thrashing of their tails in the water, and our weak minds pictured out their appalling and hideous aspects. One of my companions, the black man, took an immediate fright, and solicited me to take out the oars, and endeavour to get away from them. I consented to his using any means for that purpose; but alas! it was wholly out of our power to raise a single arm in our own defense. Two or three of the whales came down near us, and went swiftly off across our stern, blowing and spouting at a terrible rate; they, however, after an hour or two disappeared, and we saw no more of them. The next day, the 19th of January, we had extremely boisterous weather, with rain, heavy thunder and lightning, which reduced us again to the necessity of taking in all sail and lying to. The wind blew from every point of the compass within the twenty-four hours, and at last towards the next morning settled at E.N.E. a strong breeze.

January 20th. The black man, Richard Peterson, manifested today symptoms of a speedy dissolution;

he had been lying between the seats in the boat, utterly dispirited and broken down, without being able to do the least duty, or hardly to place his hand to his head for the last three days, and had this morning made up his mind to die rather than endure further misery: he refused his allowance; said he was sensible of his approaching end, and was perfectly ready to die: in a few minutes he became speechless, the breath appeared to be leaving his body without producing the least pain, and at four o'clock he was gone. I had two days previously conversations with him on the subject of religion on which he reasoned very sensibly, and with much composure; and begged me to let his wife know his fate, if ever I reached home in safety. The next morning we committed him to the sea, in latitude 35° 07′ S., longitude 105° 46′ W. The wind prevailed to the eastward until the 24th of January, when it again fell calm. We were now in a most wretched and sinking state of debility, hardly able to crawl around the boat, and possessing but strength enough to convey our scanty morsel to our mouths. When I perceived this morning that it was calm, my fortitude almost forsook me. I thought to suffer another scorching day, like the last we had experienced, would close before night the scene of our miseries; and I felt many a despairing moment that day, that had well nigh proved fatal. It required an effort to look calmly forward, and contemplate what was yet in store for us, beyond what I felt I was capable of making; and what is was that buoyed me above all the terrors which surrounded us, God alone knows. Our ounce and a half of bread, which was

to serve us all day, was in some cases greedily devoured, as if life was to continue but another moment; and at other times, it was hoarded up and
eaten crumb by crumb, at regular intervals during
the day, as if it was to last us for ever. To add to our
calamities, biles* began to break out upon us, and our
imaginations shortly became as diseased as our bodies. I laid down at night to catch a few moments of
oblivious sleep, and immediately my starving fancy
was at work. I dreamt of being placed near a splen-
did and rich repast, where there was every thing that
the most dainty appetite could desire; and of contemplating the moment in which we were to commence to eat with enraptured feelings of delight; and
just as I was about to partake of it, I suddenly awoke
to the cold realities of my miserable situation. Nothing could have oppressed me so much. It set such a
longing frenzy for victuals in my mind, that I felt
as if I could have wished the dream to continue for
ever, that I never might have awoke from it. I cast a
sort of vacant stare about the boat, until my eyes
rested upon a bit of tough cowhide, which was fastened to one of the oars; I eagerly seized and commenced to chew it, but there was no substance in it,
and it only severed to fatigue my weak jaws, and
add to my bodily pains. My fellow sufferers mur-
mured very much the whole time, and continued to
press me continually with questions upon the probability of our reaching land again. I kept constantly
rallying my spirits to enable me to afford them comfort. I encouraged them to bear up against all evils,

* Boils

and if we must perish, to die in our own cause, and
not weakly distrust the providence of the Almighty
by giving ourselves up to despair. I reasoned with
them, and told them that we would not die sooner
by keeping up our hopes; that the dreadful sacrifices and privations we endured were to preserve us
from death, and were not to be put in competition
with the price which we set upon our lives, and their
value to our families: it was, besides, unmanly to
repine at what neither admitted of alleviation nor
cure; and withal, that it was our solemn duty to rec-
ognise in our calamities an overruling divinity, by
whose mercy we might be suddenly snatched from
peril, and to rely upon him alone, "Who tempers the
wind to the shorn lamb."

The three following days, the 25th, 26th, and 27th,
were not distinguished by any particular circumstances. The wind still prevailed to the eastward,
and by its obduracy, almost tore the very hopes of
our hearts away: it was impossible to silence the
rebellious repinings of our nature, at witnessing
such a succession of hard fortune against us. It was
our cruel lot not to have had one bright anticipation
realized—not one wish of our thirsting souls gratified.
We had, at the end of these three days, been urged to
the southward as far as latitude 36° into a chilly region,
where rains and squalls prevailed; and we now calculated to tack and stand back to the northward:
after much labor, we got our boat about; and so
great was the fatigue attending this small exertion
of our bodies, that we all gave up for a moment and
abandoned her to her own course.—Not one of us

had now strength sufficient to steer, or indeed to make one single effort towards getting the sails properly trimmed, to enable us to make any headway. After an hour or two of relaxation, during which the horrors of our situation came upon us with a despairing force and effect, we made a sudden effort and got our sails into such a disposition as that the boat would steer herself; and we then threw ourselves down, awaiting the issue of time to bring us relief, or to take us from the scene of our troubles. We could now do nothing more; strength and spirits were totally gone; and what indeed could have been the narrow hopes, that in our situation, then bound us to life?

January 28th. Our spirits this morning were hardly sufficient to allow of our enjoying a change of the wind, which took place to the westward.—It had nearly become indifferent to us from what quarter it blew: nothing but the slight chance of meeting a vessel remained to us now: it was this narrow comfort alone that prevented me from lying down at once to die. But fourteen days stinted allowance of provisions remained, and it was absolutely necessary to increase the quantity to enable us to live five days longer: we therefore partook of it, as pinching necessity demanded, and gave ourselves wholly up to the guidance and disposal of our Creator.

The 29th and 30th of January, the wind continued west, and we made considerable progress until the 31st, when it again came ahead, and prostrated all our hopes. On the 1st of February, it changed again to the westward, and on the 2nd and 3rd blew to the eastward; and we had it light and variable until the 8th of February. Our sufferings were now drawing to a close; a terrible death appeared shortly to await us; hunger became violent and outrageous, and we prepared for a speedy release from our troubles; our speech and reason were both considerably impaired, and we were reduced to be at this time certainly the most helpless and wretched of the whole human race. Isaac Cole, one of our crew, had the day before this, in a fit of despair, thrown himself down in the boat, and was determined there calmly to wait for death. It was obvious that he had no chance; all was dark he said in his mind, not a single ray of hope was left for him to dwell upon; and it was folly and madness to be struggling against what appeared so palpably to be our fixed and settled destiny. I remonstrated with him as effectually as the weakness both of my body and understanding would allow of; and what I said appeared for a moment to have a considerable effect: he made a powerful and sudden effort, half rose up, crawled forward and hoisted the jib, and firmly and loudly cried that he would not give up; that he would live as long as the rest of us—but alas! this effort was but the hectic fever of the moment, and he shortly again relapsed into a state of melancholy and despair. This day his reason was attacked, and he became about 9 o'clock in the morning a most miserable spectacle of madness: he spoke incoherently about everything, calling loudly for a napkin and water, and then, lying stupidly and senselessly down in the boat again, would close his hollow eyes, as if in death. About 10 o'clock, we sudden-

ly perceived that he became speechless; we got him
as well as we were able upon a board, placed on one
of the seats of the boat, and covering him up with
some old clothes, left him to his fate. He lay in the
greatest pain and apparent misery, groaning piteous-
ly until four o'clock, when he died, in the most horrid and frightful convulsions I ever witnessed. We
kept his corpse all night, and in the morning my two
companions began as a course to make preparations
to dispose of it in the sea; when after reflecting on
the subject all night, I addressed than on the painful
subject of keeping the body for food!! Our provisions could not possibly last us beyond three days,
within which time, it was not in any degree probable
that we should find relief from our present sufferings,
and that hunger would at last drive us to the necessity
of casting lots. It was without any objection agreed
to, and we set to work as fast as we were able to prepare it so as to prevent its spoiling. We separated
his limbs from his body, and cut all the flesh from
the bones; after which, we opened the body, took out
the heart, and then closed it again—sewed it up as
decently as we could, and committed it to the sea.
We now first commenced to satisfy the immediate
cravings of nature from the heart, which we eagerly
devoured, and then ate sparingly of a few pieces of
the flesh; after which we hung up the remainder, cut
in thin strips about the boat, to dry in the sun: we
made a fire and roasted some of it, to serve us during
the next day. In this manner did we dispose of our
fellow sufferer; the painful recollection of which
brings to mind at this moment, some of the most

disagreeable and revolting ideas that it is capable
of conceiving. We knew not then to whose lot it
would fall next, either to die or be shot, and eaten
like the poor wretch we had just dispatched. Humanity must shudder at the dreadful recital. I have
no language to paint the anguish of our souls in this
dreadful dilemma. The next morning, the 10th of
February, we found that the flesh had become tainted, and had turned of a greenish color upon which
we concluded to make a fire and cook it at once, to
prevent its becoming so putrid as not to be eaten at
all: we accordingly did so, and by that means preserved it for six or seven days longer; our bread during the time remained untouched; as that would not
be liable to spoil, we placed it carefully aside for the
last moments of our trial. About three o'clock this
afternoon a strong breeze set in from the N.W. and
we made very good progress, considering that we were
compelled to steer the boat by management of the
sails alone: this wind continued until the thirteenth,
when it changed again ahead. We contrived to keep
soul and body together by sparingly partaking of our
flesh, cut up in small pieces and eaten with salt water.
By the fourteenth, our bodies became so far recruited, as to enable us to make a few attempts at guiding
our boat again with the oar; by each taking his turn,
we managed to effect it, and to make a tolerable good
course. On the fifteenth, our flesh was all consumed,
and we were driven to the last morsel of bread, consisting of two cakes; our limbs had for the last two
days swelled very much, and now began to pain us
most excessively. We were still, as near as we could

judge, three hundred miles from the land, and but three days of our allowance on hand. The hope of a continuation of the wind, which came out at west this morning, was the only comfort and solace that remained to us: so strong had our desires at last reached in this respect, that a high fever had set in, in our veins, and a longing that nothing but its continuation could satisfy. Matters were now with us at their height; all hope was cast upon the breeze; and we tremblingly and fearfully awaited its progress, and the dreadful development of our destiny. On the sixteenth, at night, full of the horrible reflections of our situation, and panting with weakness, I laid down to sleep, almost indifferent whether I should ever see the light again. I had not lain long, before I dreamt I saw a ship at some distance off from us, and strained every nerve to get to her, but could not. I awoke almost overpowered with the frenzy I had caught in my slumbers, and stung with the cruelties of a diseased and disappointed imagination. On the seventeenth, in the afternoon, a heavy cloud appeared to be settling down in an E. by N. direction from us, which in my view, indicated the vicinity of some land, which I took for the island of Mas Afuera. I concluded it could be no other; and immediately upon this reflection, the life blood began to flow again briskly in my veins. I told my companions that I was well convinced it was land, and if so, in all probability we should reach it before two days more. My words appeared to comfort them much; and by repeated assurances of the favourable appearance of things, their spirits acquired even a degree of elasticity that was truly astonishing. The dark features of our distress began now to diminish a little, and the countenance, even amid the gloomy bodings of our hard lot, to assume a much fresher hue. We directed our course for the cloud, and our progress that night was extremely good. The next morning, before daylight, Thomas Nicholson, a boy about seventeen years of age, one of my two companions who had thus far survived with me, after having bailed the boat, laid down, drew a piece of canvas over him, and cried out that he then wished to die immediately. I saw that he had given up, and I attempted to speak a few words of comfort and encouragement to him, and endeavoured to persuade him that it was a great weakness and even wickedness to abandon a reliance upon the Almighty, while the least hope, and a breath of life remained; but he felt unwilling to listen to any of the consolatory suggestions which I made to him; and, notwithstanding the extreme probability which I stated there was of our gaining the land before the end of two days more, he insisted upon lying down and giving himself up to despair. A fixed look of settled and forsaken despondency came over his face: he lay for some time silent, sullen, and sorrowful—and I felt at once satisfied that the coldness of death was fast gathering upon him: there was a sudden and unaccountable earnestness in his manner that alarmed me, and made me fear that I myself might unexpectedly be overtaken by a like weakness, or dizziness of nature, that would bereave me at once of both reason and life; but Providence willed it otherwise.

At about seven o'clock this morning, while I was lying asleep, my companion who was steering, suddenly and loudly called out *"There's a Sail!"* I know not what was the first movement I made upon hearing such an unexpected cry: the earliest of my recollections are that immediately I stood up, gazing in a state of abstraction and ecstasy upon the blessed vision of a vessel about seven miles off from us; she was standing in the same direction with us, and the only sensation I felt at the moment was, that of a violent and unaccountable impulse to fly directly towards her. I do not believe it is possible to form a just conception of the pure, strong feelings, and the unmingled emotions of joy and gratitude, that took possession of my mind on this occasion: the boy, too, took a sudden and animated start from his despondency, and stood up to witness the probable instrument of his salvation. Our only fear was now that she would not discover us, or that we might not be able to intercept her course: we, however, put our boat immediately, as well as we were able, in a direction to cut her off; and found, to our great joy, that we sailed faster than she did. Upon observing us, she shortened sail, and allowed us to come up to her. The captain hailed us, and asked who we were. I told him we were from a wreck, and he cried out immediately for us to come alongside the ship. I made an effort to assist myself along to the side, for the purpose of getting up, but strength failed me altogether, and I found it impossible to move a step further without help. We must have formed at that moment, in the eyes of the captain and his crew, a most deplorable and affecting picture of suffering and misery. Our cadaverous countenances, sunken eyes, and bones just starting through the skin, with the ragged remnants of clothes stuck about our sun burnt bodies, must have produced an appearance to him affecting and revolting in the highest degree. The sailors commenced to remove us from our boat, and we were taken to the cabin, and comfortably provided for in every respect. In a few minutes we were permitted to taste of a little thin food, made from tapioca, and in a few days, with prudent management, we were considerably recruited. This vessel proved to be the brig *Indian,* Captain William Crozier, of London; to whom we are indebted for every polite, friendly, and attentive disposition towards us, that can possibly characterize a man of humanity and feeling. We were taken up in latitude 33° 45′ S., longitude 81° 03′ W. At twelve o'clock this day we saw the island of Mas Afuera, and on the 25th of February, we arrived at Valparaiso in utter distress and poverty. Our wants were promptly relieved there.

The captain and the survivors of his boat's crew, were taken up by the American whale ship, the *Dauphin,* Captain Zimri Coffin, of Nantucket, and arrived at Valparaiso on the seventeenth of March following: he was taken up in latitude 37° S. off the island of St. Mary. The third boat got separated from him on the 28th of January, and has not been heard of since. The names of all the survivors, are as follows:—Captain George Pollard, Jr., Charles Ramsdale, Owen Chase, Benjamin Lawrence, and Thomas

Nicholson, all of Nantucket. There died in the captain's boat, the following: Brazilla Ray of Nantucket, Owen Coffin of the same place, who was shot, and Samuel Reed, a black.

The captain relates, that after being separated, as herein before stated, they continued to make what progress they could towards the island of Juan Fernandez, as was agreed upon; but contrary winds and the extreme debility of the crew prevailed against their united exertions. He was with us equally surprised and concerned at the separation that took place between us; but continued on his course, almost confident of meeting with us again. On the fourteenth, the whole stock of provisions belonging to the second mate's boat was entirely exhausted, and on the twenty-fifth, the black man, Lawson Thomas, died, and was eaten by his surviving companions. On the twenty-first, the captain and his crew were in the like dreadful situation with respect to their provisions; and on the twenty-third, another coloured man, Charles Shorter, died out of the same boat, and his body was shared for food between the crews of both boats. On the twenty-seventh, another, Isaac Shepherd, a black man, died in the third boat; and on the twenty-eighth, another black, named Samuel Reed, died out of the captain's boat. The bodies of these men constituted their only food while it lasted; and on the twenty-ninth, owing to the darkness of the night and want of sufficient power to manage their boats, those of the captain and second mate separated in latitude 35° S., longitude 100° W. On the 1st of February, having consumed the last morsel, the captain and the three other men that remained with him were reduced to the necessity of casting lots. It fell upon Owen Coffin to die, who with great fortitude and resignation submitted to his fate. They drew lots to see who should shoot him: he placed himself firmly to receive his death, and was immediately shot by Charles Ramsdale, whose hard fortune it was to become his executioner. On the 11th Brazilla Ray died; and on these two bodies the captain and Charles Ramsdale, the only two that were then left, subsisted until the morning of the twenty-third, when they fell in with the ship *Dauphin*, as before stated, and were snatched from impending destruction. Every assistance and attentive humanity, was bestowed upon them by Capt. Coffin, to whom Capt. Pollard acknowledged every grateful obligation. Upon making known the fact, that three of our companions had been left at Ducie's Island, to the captain of the U. S. frigate *Constellation*, which lay at Valparaiso when we arrived, he said he should immediately take measures to have them taken off.

On the 11th of June following I arrived at Nantucket in the whale ship the *Eagle*, Capt. William H. Coffin. My family had received the most distressing account of our shipwreck, and had given me up for lost. My unexpected appearance was welcomed with the most grateful obligations and acknowledgements to a beneficent Creator, who had guided me through darkness, trouble, and death, once more to the bosom of my country and friends.

SUPPLEMENT

The following is a list of the whole crew of the ship, with their arrangements into the three several boats upon starting from the wreck: the names of those who died, were left on the island, or shot—with those also who survived, and who were in the third or second mate's boat at the time of separation—and whose fate is yet uncertain:—

Capt. James Pollard, Jr.	1st boat	survived
Obed Hendricks,	do.	put in 3d boat*
Brazilla Ray,	do.	died
Owen Coffin,	do.	shot
Samuel Reed, (black)	do.	died
Charles Ramsdale,	do.	survived
Seth Weeks,	do.	left on the island
Owen Chase,	2d boat	survived
Benjamin Lawrence,	do.	do.
Thomas Nicholson,	do.	do.
Isaac Cole,	do.	died
Richard Peterson, (black)	do.	do.
William Wright,	do.	left on the island
Matthew P. Joy,	3d boat	died
Thomas Chapple,	do.	left on the island
Joseph West,	do.	missing
Lawson Thomas, (black)	do.	died
Charles Shorter, (black)	do.	do.
Isaiah Shepherd, (black)	do.	do.
William Bond, (black)	do.	missing

FINIS.

* Apparently should be listed as "missing," like Joseph West and William Bond.

JOURNAL

OF

VOYAGES AND TRAVELS

BY THE

Rev. DANIEL TYERMAN AND GEORGE BENNET, Esq.

DEPUTED FROM THE

LONDON MISSIONARY SOCIETY,

TO VISIT THEIR VARIOUS STATIONS

IN THE SOUTH SEA ISLANDS, CHINA, INDIA, &c.

BETWEEN THE YEARS 1821 AND 1829.

COMPILED FROM ORIGINAL DOCUMENTS,

BY JAMES MONTGOMERY,

AUTHOR OF "THE WORLD BEFORE THE FLOOD," "THE CHRISTIAN
PSALMIST," AND OTHER POEMS.

IN THREE VOLUMES.

VOL. I.

"Glorify ye the name of the Lord God of Israel in the isles of the sea.—From the
uttermost part of the earth have we heard songs, even glory to the righteous."

Isaiah xxiv. 15, 16.

From the First London Edition,
REVISED
BY AN AMERICAN EDITOR.

BOSTON:

PUBLISHED BY CROCKER AND BREWSTER,
47 Washington Street.
NEW YORK : JONATHAN LEAVITT,
182 Broadway.

1832.

CAPTAIN POLLARD'S NARRATIVE

April 16, [1823]. In the harbor here, we found the American brig *Pearl,* Captain Chandler, which had put in for repairs, having sprung a leak at sea; and on board of this vessel, to our great joy and surprise, we met with our friends, Mr. and Mrs. Chamberlain, from the Sandwich Islands. We never expected to have seen their faces again in this world. They were, however, for reasons which we had known and approved when we parted with them, on their return with their young family to America. They gave us the most gratifying account of the safe arrival and cordial reception of Mr. and Mrs. Ellis, at Oahu, by our American missionary friends there, by the king also, the chiefs, and the people—all of whom rejoiced to welcome them as servants of the Most High God, arrived among them to teach a nation, *without any religion,* the only doctrines under heaven worthy of that name.

There were three captains on board this brig, as passengers to America. The ships of two of these had been wrecked, and that of the third condemned. One of them was Captain George Pollard, whose singular and lamentable story, in the case of a *former* shipwreck (as nearly as can be recollected by Mr. Bennet), deserves to be recorded in his own manner. It was substantially as follows:—

"My first shipwreck was in open sea, on the 20th

of November, 1820, near the equator, about 118°
W. long. The vessel, a South Sea whaler, was called
the *Essex*. On that day, as we were on the look out
for sperm whales, and had actually struck two, which
the boats' crews were following to secure, I perceived
a very large one—it might be eighty or ninety feet
long—rushing with great swiftness through the water,
right towards the ship. We hoped that she would
turn aside, and dive under, when she perceived such
a balk in her way. But no! the animal came full
force against our stern-port: had any quarter less
firm been struck, the vessel must have been burst; as
it was, every plank and timber trembled throughout
her whole bulk.

"The whale, as though hurt by a severe and unexpected concussion, shook its enormous head, and
sheered off to so considerable a distance, that for some
time we had lost sight of her from the starboard
quarter; of which we were very glad, hoping that the
worst was over. Nearly an hour afterwards, we saw
the same fish—we had no doubt of this, from her
size, and the direction in which she came—making
again towards us. We were at once aware of our
danger, but escape was impossible. She dashed her
head this time against the ship's side, and so broke
it in that the vessel filled rapidly, and soon became
water-logged. At the second shock, expecting her to
go down, we lowered our three boats with the utmost expedition, and all hands, twenty in the whole,
got into them—seven, and seven, and six. In a little
while, as she did not sink, we ventured on board
again, and by scuttling the deck, were enabled to

get out some biscuit, beef, water, rum, two sextants, a quadrant, and three compasses. These, together with some rigging, a few muskets, powder, etc., we brought away; and, dividing the stores among our three small crews, rigged the boats as well as we could; there being a compass for each, and a sextant for two, and a quadrant for one, but neither sextant nor quadrant for the third. Then, instead of pushing away for some port, so amazed and bewildered were we, that we continued sitting in our places, gazing upon the ship as though she had been an object of the tenderest affection. Our eyes could not leave her, till, at the end of many hours, she gave a slight reel, then down she sank. No words can tell our feelings. We looked at each other—we looked at the place where she had so lately been afloat—and we did not cease to look, till the terrible conviction of our abandoned and perilous situation roused us to exertion, if deliverance were yet possible.

"We now consulted about the course which it might be best to take—westward to India, eastward to South America, or south-westward to the Society Isles. We knew that we were at no great distance from Tahiti, but were so ignorant of the state and temper of the inhabitants, that we feared we should be devoured by cannibals, if we cast ourselves on their mercy. It was determined therefore to make for South America, which we computed to be more than two thousand miles distant. Accordingly we steered eastward, and though for several days harrassed with squalls, we contrived to keep together. It was not long before we found that one of the boats had started a plank, which was no wonder, for whale-boats are all clinker-built, and very slight, being made of half-inch plank only, before planing. To remedy this alarming defect, we all turned to, and, having emptied the damaged boat into the two others, we raised her side as well as we could, and succeeded in restoring the plank at the bottom. Through this accident, some of our biscuit had become injured by the salt-water. This was equally divided among the several boats' crews. Food and water, meanwhile, with our utmost economy, rapidly failed. Our strength was exhausted, not by abstinence only, but by the labors which we were obliged to employ to keep our little vessels afloat, amidst the storms which repeatedly assailed us. One night we were parted in rough weather; but though the next day we fell in with one of our companion-boats, we never saw or heard any more of the other, which probably perished at sea being without either sextant or quadrant.

"When we were reduced to the last pinch, and out of everything, having been more than three weeks abroad, we were cheered with the sight of a low uninhabited island, which we reached in hope, but were bitterly disappointed. There were some barren bushes, and many rocks on this forlorn spot. The only provisions that we could procure were a few birds and their eggs: this supply was soon reduced; the sea-fowls appeared to have been frightened away, and their nests were left empty after we had once or twice plundered them. What distressed us most was the utter want of fresh water; we could not find a drop anywhere, till, at the extreme verge of ebb tide, a small spring was discovered in the sand; but even that was too scanty to afford us sufficient to quench our thirst before it was covered by the waves at their turn.

"There being no prospect but that of starvation here, we determined to put to sea again. Three of our comrades, however, chose to remain, and we pledged ourselves to send a vessel to bring them off, if we ourselves should ever escape to a Christian port. With a very small morsel of biscuit for each, and a little water, we again ventured out on the wide ocean. In the course of a few days, our provisions were consumed. Two men died; we had no other alternative than to live upon their remains. These we roasted to dryness by means of fires kindled on the ballast-sand at the bottom of the boats. When this supply was spent, what could we do? We looked at each other with horrid thoughts in our minds, but we held our tongues. I am sure that we loved one another as brothers all the time; and yet our looks told plainly what must be done. We cast lots, and the fatal one fell on my poor cabin-boy. I started forward instantly, and cried out, 'My lad, my lad, *if you don't like your lot,* I'll shoot the first man that touches you.' The poor emaciated boy hesitated a moment or two; then, quietly laying his head down upon the gunnel of the boat, he said, '*I like it as well as any other.*' He was soon dispatched, and nothing of him left. I think, then, another man died of himself, and him, too, we ate. But I can tell you no more—my head is on fire at the recollection; I hardly know what I say.

I forgot to say, that we had parted company with the second boat before now. After some more days of horror and despair, when some were lying down at the bottom of the boat, not able to rise, and scarcely one of us could move a limb, a vessel hove in sight. We were taken on board, and treated with extreme kindness. The second lost boat was also picked up at sea, and the survivors saved. A ship afterwards sailed in search of our companions on the desolate island, and brought them away."

Captain Pollard closed his dreary narrative with saying, in a tone of despondency never to be forgotten by him who heard it—"After a time I found my way to the United States, to which I belonged, and got another ship. That, too, I have lost by a second wreck off the Sandwich Islands, and now I am utterly ruined. No owner will ever trust me with a whaler again, for all will say I am an *unlucky* man."*

---

* This last paragraph was unaccountably dropped from the American edition.

AN ACCOUNT

OF THE

LOSS OF THE ESSEX,

FROM

HAVING BEEN STRUCK BY A WHALE IN THE SOUTH SEAS
WITH SOME INTERESTING PARTICULARS OF
THE SUFFERINGS OF HER CREW ON A DESERT ISLAND
AND IN THEIR BOATS AT SEA.

FROM THE NARRATIVE OF ONE OF THE SURVIVORS

LONDON:

Printed for

THE RELIGIOUS TRACT SOCIETY,

Instituted 1799 ;

AND SOLD AT THEIR DEPOSITORY, 56, PATERNOSTER-ROW ; BY
J. AND C. EVANS, 42, LONG-LANE ; AND BY OTHER
BOOKSELLERS.

[*Price One Penny.*]

LOSS OF THE *ESSEX*

THE ship *Essex*, George Pollard, Master, sailed from Nantucket, in North America, August 12, 1819,* on a whaling voyage to the South Seas.

The *Essex* was for some months very successful, and procured 750 barrels of oil, in a shorter period than usual.

On the 20th November, 1820, she was on the equator, about 118° west longitude, when several whales were in sight, to the great joy of the crew, who thought they should soon complete their cargo.

The boats were soon lowered in pursuit of the whales: George Pollard, the master, and Thomas Chapple, the second mate, each succeeded in striking one, and were actively engaged in securing them, when a black man, who was in the mate's boat, exclaimed, "Massa, where ship?" The mate immediately looked round, and saw the *Essex* lying on her beam ends, and a large whale near her: he instantly cut his line and made towards the ship; the captain also saw what had happened and did the same. As soon as they got on board, to their great astonishment they found she had been struck by a whale of the largest size, which rose close to the ship and then darted under her, and knocked off a great part of the false keel. The whale appeared again, and went about a quarter of a mile off, then suddenly returned and struck the ship with great force. The shock was most

---

* In the original, the date is incorrectly given as November 19, 1819.

violent, the bows were stove in, and the vessel driven astern a considerable distance; she filled with water and fell over on her beam ends. The crew exerted themselves to the utmost, the masts were cut away and the ship righted, but she was a mere wreck and entirely unmanageable; the quantity of oil on board alone kept her from foundering. They did not ascertain whether the whale received any injury, but it remained in sight for some hours without again coming near them.

When the captain found that it was impossible to save the ship, he directed the three boats to be got ready, and they succeeded in saving a small quantity of water, and some biscuit, which was in a very wet state.

As the *Essex* appeared likely to float for some days longer, the captain remained by her, hoping that some vessel might come in sight. After three days, finding these hopes were not realized, as the wind blew fresh from the east, he determined on attempting the Friendly [Tonga] Islands. They accordingly steered a south-westerly course, and proceeded rapidly for twenty-three days without seeing land. During this time they had only half a biscuit and a pint of water each man, per day; in that warm climate the scanty supply of water was particularly distressing, but they could not venture on a larger allowance; as on leaving the ship their whole stock of provisions was only about one hundred and fifty pounds of bread and fifty gallons of water; occasionally, however, some showers of rain fell, which gave them considerable relief.

On the twenty-fouth day after leaving the *Essex* they saw an island, discovered a few years since, and called Elizabeth's Isle [Henderson Island]. It is about eight or nine miles round, low and flat, nearly covered with trees and underwood.

The shore was rocky and the surf high; the crew were very weak, so that they did not land without considerable difficulty. Their first search was for water; and their joy was great at finding a spring of fresh water among the rocks; they were, however, disappointed on examining the island, as it was almost destitute of the necessaries of life, and no other fresh water could be discoverd. These painful feelings were greatly increased the following day, for the sea had flowed over the rocks, and the spring of fresh water could not be seen, and did not again appear. In this extremity they endeavoured to dig wells, but without success; their only resource was a small quantity of water which they found in some holes among the rocks.

For six days they continued to examine the island, when finding their situation desperate, the captain and most of the crew determined to put to sea again. The continent of South America was seventeen hundred miles distant, and in their destitute condition they could scarcely expect to reach land: their hopes were rather directed to the possibility of falling in with some vessel.

Thomas Chapple, the second mate, being in a very weak state, thought he might as well remain on the island, as attempt such a voyage; William Wright and Seth Weeks also determined to remain with him.

On the 26th of December the boats left the island: this was indeed a trying moment to all: they separated with mutual prayers and good wishes, seventeen venturing to sea with almost certain death before them, while three remained on a rocky isle, destitute of water, and affording hardly any thing to support life. The prospects of these three poor men were gloomy: they again tried to dig a well but without success, and all hope seemed at an end, when providentially they were relieved by a shower of rain. They were thus delivered from the immediate apprehension of perishing by thirst. Their next care was to procure food, and their difficulties herein were also very great; their principal resource was small birds, about the size of a blackbird, which they caught while at roost. Every night they climbed the trees in search of them, and obtained, by severe exertions, a scanty supply, hardly enough to support life. Some of the trees bore a small berry which gave them a little relief, but these they found only in small quantities. Shell-fish they searched for in vain; and although from the rocks they saw at times a number of sharks, and also other sorts of fish, they were unable to catch any, as they had no fishing tackle. Once they saw several turtles, and succeeded in taking five, but they were then without water; at those times they had little inclination to eat, and before one of them was quite finished the others were become unfit for food.

Their sufferings from want of water were the most severe, their only supply being from what remained in holes among the rocks after the showers which fell at intervals; and sometimes they were five or six days without any; on these occasions they were compelled to suck the blood of the birds they caught, which allayed their thirst in some degree; but they did so unwillingly, as they found themselves much disordered thereby.

Among the rocks were several caves formed by nature, which afforded a shelter from the wind and rain. In one of these caves they found eight human skeletons, in all probability the remains of some poor mariners who had been shipwrecked on the isle, and perished for want of food and water. They were side by side, as if they had laid down, and died together! This sight deeply affected the mate and his companions; their case was similar, and they had every reason to expect ere long the same end; for many times they lay down at night, with their tongues swollen and their lips parched with thirst, scarcely hoping to see the morning sun; and it is impossible to form an idea of their feelings when the morning dawned, and they found their prayers had been heard and answered by a providential supply of rain.

In this state they continued till the 5th of April following; day after day hoping some vessel might touch at the island; but day after day, and week after week passed by, and they continued in that state of anxious expectation which always tends to cast down the mind and damp exertion, and which is so strongly expressed in the words of Scripture, "Hope deferred maketh the heart sick." The writer of this narrative says: "At this time I found religion not

only useful but absolutely necessary to enable me to
bear up under these severe trials. If any man wishes
for happiness in this world or in the world to come,
he can only find it by belief in God and trust in him:
it is particularly important that seamen whose troubles and dangers are so numerous should bear this in
mind. In this situation we prayed earnestly, morning, noon, and night, and found comfort and support
from thus waiting upon the Lord."

This testimony of the benefits to be derived from
religion is exceedingly valuable: hours of trial prove
the vanity and uncertainty of all earthly enjoyments,
and show the necessity of looking forward for another and a better world. The experience of believers
of old taught them that they were but "strangers and
pilgrims upon earth," and led them to earnest desires after another and a better country, that is, an
heavenly. (See Heb. xi.) Prayer is the means which
God has appointed whereby we may draw near to
him, asking for the blessings we need. He has promised to hear and to answer us in such a manner as
shall be for our good: but let us always remember,
that prayer does not consist in merely kneeling down,
and uttering our desires with our lips, but prayer
should be the earnest expression of the feelings of the
heart, filled with a sense of its own misery and wretch-
edness, not only as to the things of this life, but still
more deeply affected as to the concerns of our souls.
We may be miserable in this world and in the world
to come also.—We may be happy in this life and miserable hereafter. The one does not depend upon
the other, nor are they in any way connected with

each other. The prayer of the poor publican (as related in the 18th of St. Luke) was, "God be merciful to me a sinner!" This will always be the first and principal desire of the soul, when awakened to a knowledge of its wretched and miserable state by nature and practice, and we would hope that such was the prayer of these poor men. Our Saviour himself has promised, that he will hear and answer such prayers: he graciously declares, "Come unto me all ye that labor and are heavy laden, and I will give you rest." He has also promised that he will give his Holy Spirit to those that ask him; and the soul that is led by the teaching of the Holy Spirit to draw near to the Saviour will find support under all the troubles of this life. It will find that peace which the world cannot give.

To return to these poor men. On the morning of April 5th, 1820, they were in the woods as usual, searching for food and water, as well as their weakness permitted, when their attention was aroused by a sound which they thought was distant thunder, but looking towards the sea, they saw a ship in the offing, which had just fired a gun. Their joy at this sight may be more easily imagined than described: they immediately fell on their knees and thanked God for his goodness, in thus sending deliverance when least expected; then hastening to the shore, they saw a boat coming towards them. As the boat could not approach the shore without great danger, the mate being a good swimmer, and stronger than his companions, plunged into the sea, and narrowly escaped a watery grave at the moment when deliverance was at hand; but the same Providence which had hitherto protected, now preserved him. His companions crawled out further on the rocks, and by the great exertions of the crew were taken into the boat, and soon found themselves on board the *Surry*, commanded by Captain Raine. They were treated in the kindest manner by him and his whole crew, and their health and strength were speedily restored, so that they were able to assist in the duties of the ship.

When on board the *Surry*, they were told the deplorable and painful history of their captain and shipmates. After leaving the isle, the boats parted company; the captain's boat was sixty days at sea, when it was picked up by an American whaler: only himself and a boy were then alive. There scanty stock of provisions was soon exhausted, and life had only been sustained by the dead bodies of their companions. The particulars of their sufferings are too painful to relate, but they were confirmed by proofs which could not be doubted. The ship reached Valparaiso in a few days; when the particulars of the loss of the *Essex* and of the men left on the island were immediately communicated to the captain of an American frigate then in the port; who humanely endeavoured to procure a vessel to go to the island, as his own ship was not ready for sea. Captain Raine, of the *Surry*, engaged to do this, and sailed without loss of time: he had a quick passage; and, by the kind providence of God, the mate and his companions were preserved till thus unexpectedly relieved.

The sufferings of these men were great, and their preservation remarkable: such circumstances afford instruction to every one. If you are inclined to say, there is no probability of your being similarly situated, remember that although not placed in a desert island, or in a small boat, destitute of the means of subsistence, yet all are placed in the midst of many and great dangers, as to this life. But it is of infinitely more importance to remember that there is a great and awful danger, namely, of eternal death, to which we are all alike exposed, if ignorant of the Saviour and his salvation. The subject speaks *both* to seamen and landmen: are you aware of its importance? Pray earnestly to God for the knowledge of his truth: these men prayed earnestly for deliverance from their sufferings: and can you be less earnest respecting your soul? Again, remember that God has promised to give his Holy Spirit to those that ask, and it is only by his teaching that we can be led to a knowledge of our danger, and of the value of that salvation which is so fully and freely offered unto us, through Christ, who died for our sins, and rose again for our justification.

To return to our narrative. The mate and two survivors of his boat's crew were picked up by another ship, after sufferings similar to those of the captain; but the third boat was never heard of, and its crew are supposed to have perished for want, or to have found a watery grave.

The *Surry* proceeded to New South Wales and the mate, Mr. Chapple, returned to London, in June, 1823, and furnished the details from which this account has been drawn up. He says, "Before I was cast away, I was like most seamen, I never thought much about religion; but no man has seen more of the goodness of the Lord than I have, or had more reason to believe in Him. I trust I am enabled to do so." He also bears a strong testimony to the good resulting from the labors of the missionaries in the islands of the South Sea, and the great change effected in the natives; he says, "There are very many among the poor natives of those isles, who know more of religion, and show more of the effects of it in their conduct, than the greater part of our own countrymen."

We meet with many instances of unexpected dangers and remarkable preservations, but few are more worthy of notice than the one which has been related. May they lead the reader to a more earnest and constant attendance upon the means of Divine grace. Above all, remember, that it is not merely hearing of Divine truths, or bending the knees in prayer, that can save from the sentence of "Depart ye cursed"; which will be pronounced at the last day on all evil and wicked doers: nothing but feeling, deeply feeling, our lost and ruined state by nature, the evil of sin, and the necessity of a change of heart, can lead us to look to the Saviour, and to trust in him for pardon and salvation.

Again, remember that ALL, whether seamen or landsmen, are passing rapidly along and hastening to Eternity! ETERNITY! *solemn,* awful word! *Fearful* to those who are pursuing a course of sin and folly, but *delightful* to the believer in the Lord Jesus Christ; who has been brought out of nature's darkness into marvellous light, and from the power of sin and

Satan, to rejoice in the God of salvation; having obtained pardon and sanctification by the blood of the cross, through the influence of the Holy Spirit. And though the believer's course through life may be across a stormy and tempestuous ocean, yet he proceeds with confidence, assured that he shall reach his desired port in safety, because Christ is his pilot and Saviour.

NOTE ON MELVILLE'S MEMORANDA ON OWEN CHASE

Sometime around April of 1851, as he was winding down with the writing of *Moby Dick,* Herman Melville received a copy of Chase's narrative from his father-in-law, Judge Lemuel Shaw. Melville's memoranda, entitled "What I know of Owen Chace & c," are on numbered pages in this volume, apparently sewn in when the defective copy was rebound. Melville's copy of the narrative, as noted on page twenty-one of the memoranda, was missing several pages from the conclusion (the last six pages of the 128-page narrative). Of the pages in the memoranda itself, which were written on light blue paper, the sheets numbered one and eight through thirteen are blank, and sheets nineteen and twenty have been torn out.

Melville seems to have written the memoranda, titled and untitled, at different times, and he may have left sheets blank with the intention of filling in further information relating to Chase, Captain Pollard, and the narrative. The volume, today housed in the Houghton Library at Harvard University, contains as well a note from Thomas Macy to Shaw that reads:

Hon. Lemuel Shaw
    Herewith I send thee a mutilated copy of the *Narrative of the Loss of the Ship Essex of Nantucket.* I should not have

sent this imperfect copy, [for] the fact, that this is the only copy that I have been able to procure—

Respectfully thy friend
Thos. Macy
Nantucket 4 M 1851

THE correspondence surrounding Melville's acquisition of the book suggests that he requested the narrative in large part because of the precedent the story provides for a whale sinking a ship. His long-term fascination with Chase is clear from the memoranda itself. Melville scholars have demonstrated that Melville could not have seen Owen Chase at sea in 1841, as he describes on page five of the memoranda, since Chase had retired in 1840 (and in that year received a divorce presided over by Judge Shaw himself).

For thorough discussions of these and other historical details relating to the memoranda, see the Northwestern University–Newberry Library edition of *Moby Dick,* edited by Harrison Hayford, Hershel Parker, and G. Thomas Tanselle (1988) and Thomas Heffernan's *Stove by a Whale: Owen Chase and the Essex* (1981). Both of these editions reprint facsimiles of the memoranda along with transcriptions. Melville's handwriting is at times difficult to decipher, and these transcriptions differ slightly from each other, and in a few cases from the transcription that follows.

General Evidence "

This thing of the Essex is found (stupidly altercated) in many compilations of nautical adventure made within the last 15 or 20 years. TP. the Englishman Bennet in his exact work ("Whaling Voyage round the Globe") quotes the thing as an acknowledged fact.

TP. Besides seamen some landsman (Judge Shaw & others) acquainted with Nantucket, have evinced to me their unquestioning faith in the thing; having seen Captain Pollard himself, & been conversant with his situation in Nantucket since the disaster

What I know of Owen Chace
&c

When I was on board
the ship Acushnet of Fairhaven,
in the passage to the Pacific
cruising-grounds, among other
matters of forecastle conversation at times was
the story of the Essex. It
was then that I first
became acquainted
with her history and her
truly astounding fate.

But what there
served to specialize my
interest at the time was
the circumstance that the

4 Second mate of our ship.
Mr Hall, an Englishman
& Londoner by birth, had
for two three-years voyages
sailed with Owen Chace (then
in command of the whale
ship "William Wirt" (I think
it was) of Nantucket.) This
Hall always spoke of Chace
with much interest & sincere
regard — but he did not
seem to know any thing
more about him or the
Essex affair than any body
else. ⁂. See p. 19. of M.S.

Somewhere about the
latter part of A. D. 1841
in this same ship the
Acushnet, we spoke the

Wm. Wirt" of Nantucket, & Owen Chace was the Captain, & so it came to pass that I saw him. He was a large, powerful well-made man; rather tall; to all appearance something past forty-five or so; with a handsome face for a Yankee, & expressive of great sprightliness & calm unostentatious courage. His whole appearance impressed me pleasantly. He was the most prepossessing-looking whale-hunter I think I ever saw.

—— Being a mere foremast-hand I had no opportunity of conversing with Owen (tho' he was

on board our ship for two
hours at a time) nor have
I ever seen him since.

But I should have
before mentioned, that before
seeing Chace's ship, we
spoke another Nantucket
craft & gammed with her.
On the forecastle I made
the acquaintance of a fine
lad of sixteen or
thereabouts, a son of
Owen Chace. I questioned
him concerning his father's
adventure; and when I
left his ship to return
again the next morning (for
the two vessels were to sail
in company for a few days)

he went to his desk &
handed me a complete
copy (same edition as this
one) of the Narrative.
This was the first printed
account of it I had ever
seen, & the only copy of
Chase's Narrative (regular &
authentic) except the present
one. The reading of this
wondrous story upon the
landless sea, & close to the
very latitude of the shipwreck
had a surprising effect upon me.

Authorship of the Book

There seems no reason to
suppose that Owen himself
wrote the narrative. It
bears obvious tokens of having
been written for him; but
at the same time, its whole
air plainly evinces that it
was carefully & consecutively
written to Owen's dictation
of the facts. — It is
almost as good as tho' Owen
wrote it himself.

Another Narrative
of the Adventure
"

I have been told that
Pollard the captain, wrote,
or caused to be wrote under
his own name, his version
of the story. I have seen
extract purports to be
from some such work.
But I have never seen
the work itself. — I should
imagine him chosen to have
been the fittest person to
narrate the thing.

16

<u>Note</u>

Vide ante p. p. 4 — 5 , m. s.

I was doubtful a little
at the time of writing whether
this ship was the Wm West. I am
now certain that it was the
<u>Charles Carroll</u> . of which
Owen Chace was captain
for several voyages.

Since writing the
foregoing I — somewhat
that 1850 – 3 —
saw Capt Pollard
on the island of
Nantucket, and
indulged some hours
with him. To the
extent he was a
nobody — to me,
the most

Sequel

"

I can not tell
exactly how many more pages the (6)
complete narrative contains — but
at any rate, very little more remains
to related. — The boat was
picked up by the ship, & the
two fellows were landed in Chili.
& in time sailed for home.
Owen Chace returned to his
business of whaling, & in due
time became a Captain,
as related in the beginning.

Captain Pollard's boat
(from which Chace's had become
separated) was also after
a miserable time, picked
up by a ship, but not

until two of its crew had
died delirious, & furnished
food for the survivors.

The third boat, it does
not appear, that it was ever
heard of, after its sub-separation
from Pollard's.

Pollard himself
returns to Nantucket, &
subsequently sailed on another
whaling voyage to the Pacific,
but he had not been
in the Pacific long, when
one night, his ship went
ashore on unknown rocks,
& was dashed to pieces.
The crew, with Pollard,
put off in their boats, &
were soon picked up by

and the whale - ship, with which,
the day previs, they had sailed
in company. —— I got this
from Hall, Second mate of
the Acushnet. ——

Pollard it seems,
now took the hint, & after
reaching home from this second
shipwreck, vowed to abide
ashore. He has ever
since lived in Nantucket.
Hall told me that he
became a butcher there.
I believe he is still living.
Night - Watchman Concay the three
men left on the island; —
they were taken off at last
(in a sad state enough
enough) by a ship, which

purposely touched there for them,
being advised of them, by their
shipmates who had been-
opportunely landed by the sh
in Chili.

—————— All the sufferings
of these miserable men of the
Essex might, on all human
probability, have been avoided,
had they, immediately after leaving
the wreck, steered straight
for Tahiti; from which they
were not very distant at
the time, & to which, there
was a fair Trade wind.
But they dreaded cannibals,
& ships to tell knew
not that for more than
'20 years, the English

missions had been sent in
Tahiti; & that in the same
epoch of the shipwreck —1820—
it was entirely safe for the
sharers to touch at Tahiti.
—— But they chose to
steer a head wind, & make
a passage of some thousand
miles (an unwisely
roundabout one, too) in order
to form a circuitous harbour
on the coast of South America.

Further
Concerning Owen Chace

The miserable portion
acidous of misfortune which
pursued Pollard the Captain,
in his second disasters
& entire shipwreck, did
likewise hunt poor Owen,
tho' somewhat more
dilatory in overtaking
him the second time.
For, while I was
in the Acushnet we
heard from some whale-
ship that we spoke, that
the Captain of the "Charles

Carrol" — that is Owen Chace —
had recently received letters
from home, informing him of
the certain unfidelity of his
wife, the mother of several
children, one of them being the
lad of sixteen, whom I
alluded to as giving me
a copy of his father's
narrative to read. He
also heard that this receipt
of this news had told
most heavily upon Chace,
& that he was a prey to
the deepest gloom.

[2]   General Evidences

This thing of the Essex is found (stupidly abbreviated) in many compilations of nautical adventure made within the last 15 or 20 years.

The Englishman Bennett in his exact work ("Whaling Voyage round the Globe") quotes the thing as an acknowledged fact.

Besides seamen, some landsmen (Judge Shaw & others) acquainted with Nantucket, have evinced to me their unquestioning faith in the thing; having seen Captain Pollard himself, & being conversant with his situation in Nantucket since the disaster.

[3]   What I know of Owen Chace etc.

When I was on board the ship Acushnet of Fairhaven, on the passage to the Pacific cruising-grounds, among other matters of forecastle conversation at times was the story of the Essex. It was then that I first became acquainted with her history and her truly astounding fate.

But what then served to specialize my interest at the time was the circumstance that the [4] Second mate of our ship, Mr. Hall, an Englishman & Londoner by birth, had for two three-years voyages sailed with Owen Chace (then in command of the whaleship "William* Wirt" (I think it was) of Nantucket.) This Hall always spoke of Chace with much interest & sincere regard—but he did not seem to know anything more about him or the Essex affair than anybody else. *See p. 19. of M.S.

Somewhere about the latter part of A.D. 1841, in this same ship the Acushnet, we spoke the [5] "Wm. Wirt*" of Nantucket & Owen Chace was the Captain, & so it came to pass that I saw him. He was a large, powerful well-made man; rather tall; to all appearances something past forty-five or so; with a handsome face for a Yankee, & expressive of great uprightness & calm unostentatious courage. His whole appearance (?) impressed me pleasurably (?). He was the most prepossessing-looking whale-hunter I think I ever saw.

Being a mere (?) foremast-hand I had no opportunity of conversing with Owen (tho' he was [6] on board our ship for two hours at a time) nor have I ever seen him since.

But I should have before mentioned, that before seeing Chace's ship, we spoke another Nantucket craft & *gammed* with her. In the forecastle I made the acquaintance of a fine lad of sixteen or thereabouts, a son of Owen Chace. I questioned him concerning his father's adventure; and when I left his ship to return again the next morning (for the two vessels were to sail in company for a few days) [7] he went to his chest & handed me a complete copy (same edition as this one) of the *Narrative*. This was the first printed account of it I had ever seen, & the only copy of Chace's Narrative (regular & authentic) except the present one. The reading of this wondrous (?) story upon the landless sea, & close to the very latitude of the shipwreck had a surprising effect upon me.

[14]   Authorship of the Book
There seems no reason to suppose that Owen himself wrote the Narrative. It bears obvious tokens of
having been written for him; but at the same time,
its whole air plainly evinces that it was carefully &
conscientiously (?) written to Owen's dictation of
the facts.—It is almost as good as tho' Owen wrote it
himself.

[15]   Another Narrative
                 of the Adventure
I have been told that Pollard the Captain, wrote,
or caused to be wrote under his own name, his version of the story. I have seen extracts purporting to
be from some such work. But I have never seen the
work itself.—I should imagine Owen Chace to have
been the fittest person to narrate the thing.

[16]   Note
                 Vide ante p.p. 4-5, m.s.
I was doubtful a little at the time of writing whether this ship was the Wm. Wirt. I am now certain that
it was the *Charles Carroll* of which Owen Chace was
captain for several voyages.

[17] Since writing the foregoing I—sometime about
1850-3—saw Capt. Pollard on the island of Nantucket, and exchanged (?) some words (?) with him.
To the islanders he was a nobody—to me, the most
[18] impressive man, tho' wholly unassuming, even
humble—that I ever encountered.

[21]   Legend
I can not tell exactly how many more pages the
complete narrative contains—but at any rate, very

little more remains to be related.—The boat was
picked up by the ship, & the poor fellows were landed in Chili & in June sailed for home. Owen Chace
returned to his business of whaling, & in due time
became a Captain, as related in the beginning.

Captain Pollard's boat (from which Chace's had
become separated) was also after a miserable time,
picked up by a ship, but not [22] until two of its
crew had died delirious, & furnished food for the
survivors.

The third boat, it does not appear, that it was
ever heard of, after its sub-separation from Pollard's.

Pollard himself returned to Nantucket, & subsequently sailed on another whaling voyage to the
Pacific, but he had not been in the Pacific long, when
one night, his ship went ashore on unknown rocks,
& was dashed to pieces. The crew, with Pollard,
put off in their boats, & were soon picked up by [23]
another whale-ship, with which, the day previous,
they had sailed in company.—I got this from Hall,
Second mate of the Acushnet.

Pollard, it seems, now took the hint & after reaching home from this second shipwreck, vowed to
abide ashore. He has ever since lived in Nantucket.
Hall told me that he became a butcher there. I believe he is still living. *A night watchman.*

Concerning the three men left on the island;—
they were taken off at last (in a sad state enough) by
a ship, which [24] purposely touched there for them,
being advised of them, by their shipmates who had
been previously landed in Chili.

All the sufferings of these miserable men of the

Essex might, in all human probability, have been avoided had they, immediately after leaving the wreck, steered straight for Tahiti, from which they were not very distant at the time, & to which, there was a fair Trade wind. But they dreaded cannibals, & strange to tell knew not that for more than 20 years, the English [25] missionaries (?) had been resident in Tahiti; & that in the same year of the ship-wreck—1820—it was entirely safe for the Marin (Mar-iners?) to touch at Tahiti.

But they chose to stem a head wind, & make a passage of several thousand miles (an unavoidably (?) roundabout one too) in order to gain a civilized (?) harbor on the coast of South America.

[26]   Further
            Concerning Owen Chace

The miserable pertinaciousness of misfortune which pursued Pollard the Captain, in his second disaster & entire shipwreck did likewise hunt poor Owen, tho' somewhat more dilatory in overtaking him the second time.

For, while I was in the Acushnet we heard from some whale-ship that we spoke, that the Captain of the *"Charles* [27] *Carroll"*—that is Owen Chace—had recently received letters from home, informing him of the certain infidelity of his wife, the mother of several children, one of them being the lad of sixteen, whom I alluded to as giving me a copy of his father's narrative to read.[1] We also heard that this receipt of this news had told most heavily upon Chace, & that he was a prey (?) to the deepest gloom.

1 Melville was unaware that it was Chase's third wife who was unfaithful.